248.8
L81/541

AUTHOR

Lucas of St Joseph Father OCD

TITLE

The Secret of the Sanctity
of St John of the Cross

DATE DUE	BORROWER'S NAME

248.8

248.8
L81/
541

THE SECRET OF SANCTITY OF
ST. JOHN OF THE CROSS

The
SECRET
of
SANCTITY
of
ST. JOHN *of the* CROSS

By **FATHER LUCAS OF ST. JOSEPH, O.C.D.**

Translated by **SISTER MARY ALBERTO, C.S.J.**
Sisters of St. Joseph, Boston, Mass.

THE BRUCE PUBLISHING COMPANY • *Milwaukee*

NIHIL OBSTAT:

Bruno Cocuzzi, O.C.D.
Alphonse Healy, O.C.D.

IMPRIMI POTEST:

Christopher Latimer, O.C.D.
Provincial of the Immaculate Heart Province

NIHIL OBSTAT:

John F. Murphy, S.T.D.
Censor librorum

IMPRIMATUR:

✠ William E. Cousins
Archbishop of Milwaukee
February 23, 1962

Library of Congress Catalog Card Number: 62–13664

PREFACE

At a time when materialism is prevalent in both the spiritual and secular world we find ourselves continually seeking a remedy for the evil. It is precisely with this in mind that readers will welcome this translation of one of the outstanding, but not so well-known works of the mystical doctor, St. John of the Cross. Although the work was originally written some four centuries ago the spiritual counsels are just as applicable to present-day situations as they were then. Essentially the same problems and temptations face those desirous of obtaining perfection, regardless of time or circumstance, and so with remarkable vision, St. John has given the solution to many of man's problems.

Primarily these counsels were given in conference form to a group of nuns in Beas, Andalucia. Later they were written into spiritual treatises known as the *Cautelas* or "Counsels to Religious." This was done by the saint himself embellishing many of the basic ideas given in conference. Few copies of the original have survived so it is not surprising to find that at least some of the original text and meaning has been lost through translation and revision. The present edition is a revised translation of the work entitled *La Santidad en el Claustro* or *Holiness in the Cloister*.

It is not sufficient for the reader to make a perfunctory or casual reading of these counsels to obtain their greatest benefit; rather he must make a profound and meditative study of the work in order to discover himself as he truly stands in the eyes of God. None of these counsels are to be considered merely in the abstract; to do so would be to create a rigid formality never intended by the author. Rather they should be considered as the practical choice between the love and will of God in relation to the love and gratification of self. The knowledge thus obtained should, with the grace of God, supply the necessary impetus for obtaining greater perfection in this life which will lead to a more perfect and closer union with God for all eternity.

CONTENTS

THE SECRET OF SANCTITY OF
ST. JOHN OF THE CROSS

CHAPTER ONE

THE CARMELITE HERITAGE

In the Acts of the Apostles we read of St. Paul's working great miracles on the sick by the simple invocation of the name of Jesus. In great admiration, the Jews, intent on curing those possessed of an evil spirit, likewise invoked the name of Jesus saying, "I adjure you by the Jesus, whom Paul preaches. . . ."[1] Foremost among those who attempted this form of exorcism were the seven sons of Esceva. While in the process of exorcising a man overcome with the evil spirit the devil indignantly addressed them thus: "Jesus, I acknowledge, and Paul I know; but who are you?"[2] Whereupon the devil caused the man to attack his exorcists with such fury that they fled from the scene in terror. St. John of the Cross makes the following commentary on this biblical passage:

"This failure to drive out the evil spirit on the part of the sons of Esceva was due to their not possessing the necessary qualifications for exorcism. God is greatly offended by those who teach the law and do not observe it themselves. To quote St. Paul: 'Thou therefore who teachest another, dost thou not teach thyself?'[3] The Holy Ghost speaking through David says to the sinner: 'Why dost thou proclaim my justices and speak of upholding my law? Seeing thou hast hated discipline and hast cast my words behind thee!' "[4]

It is, therefore, both dangerous and meaningless for one to attempt to perform the works of God if he is not completely possessed of the spirit of God.

We Carmelites have many external titles in which we justly glory. We belong to a celebrated order, whose saints, founders, and reformers are matchless and whose glories are unprecedented. It is evident, then, that our dignity and even our salvation demand of us continuous efforts so that our interior spirit will be in complete conformity to these external glories. It would indeed be a disgrace if in all truth and justice these words could be applied to any

1

religious: "We know the evangelical counsels you profess and the religious order to which you belong; we respect the habit which you wear, but if you did not bear the name of the order to which you profess to belong, we would know you not. We do not know by what authority you speak to us of the very things you yourselves do not imitate."

Yet even such a condemnation as this would not constitute the greatest of evil because a habit could be esteemed and saints venerated by men who do not and cannot penetrate the innermost recesses of the human heart. Such opinions are merely the expression of the judgments formed by what appears to the senses since interior motives are judged by exterior performances. Thus the wearing of a religious habit will avail us little if we fail to live an interior life. The all-searching eye of God penetrates into the deepest corners of the human soul, where man is revealed as he is; where the actions of men are judged in conformity with the voice of his conscience. Not even the minutest motive or action can escape the all-knowing God.

It is possible that at times a man's conscience may fail to admonish him of a wrong and such an act will not be condemned by God, any more than anyone who has not reached the use of reason will be rewarded for good works which have not been approved of by his conscience. It follows, then, that man is before the eyes of God precisely as he is revealed in the light of his own right conscience. Therefore, to realize one's true spiritual condition it is necessary to attend to the dictates and revelations of conscience and not to the opinion of one's neighbor.

Certainly much more is to be expected of a religious than of a virtuous person in the world. Of such a soul which has received countless blessings and graces from God, St. Theresa says: "Thousands of eyes are watching the soul favored by God, just as thousands of ordinary souls remain unseen. The soul which has been given great gifts must be prepared for the counteracting force of martyrdom because the world will not tolerate the slightest imperfection or blemish on those whom they consider especially favored by God. Rather, its very complaints and demands will serve the impetus for this martyrdom and advance in perfection."[5] Unless a special grace is given by God, perfection is not the acquisition of a few moments, nor does God require an immediate perfection; he is delighted with the soul's continued desire to serve Him and thus obtain a closer union. On the other hand, the world does not allow for the slightest deviation from the path of virtue and oftentimes it may account something as a fault which in itself may be considered a meritorious act before God.

It is not sufficient that a religious follow the dictates of his conscience merely as a human being, or even a Christian. His obligations are far greater because God will not judge him according to the standards of his fellow Christians but rather according to the conditions implied by his membership in a particular religious order to which he has been called by God and in which he has vowed to serve Him. While sanctity and perfection have one and the same end, God, the means of achieving that end are varied and many. Thus what may be excellent for the members of one religious order may not be the road of perfection for another order at all. The individual perfection consists primarily in imitating the sublime model of perfection, Christ, and in perfect conformity to the will of God as revealed through the spirit and rules of the particular congregation one has embraced, freely and willingly, for the love of God. Christ has said, "Be you . . . perfect as also your heavenly Father is perfect . . ."[6] but He has likewise said, "In my Father's house there are many mansions."[7] These mansions refer to the varied degrees of perfection which each is called upon to realize by virtue of his vocation and to which God has attached graces which are peculiar to that individual vocation and no other. Without a perfect understanding and realization of this truth all our greatest efforts will avail us nothing. The great apostle Paul verifies this when he states that God wishes us to be sanctified according to the state to which He, in His mercy, has called us. It was for this very reason that God has enriched the various founders of religious orders with virtues which are predominant in their order and which they exemplify so they may serve as perfect models to their followers. "Be ye followers of me and walk along the road to perfection in the way I have taught you."[8]

St. Theresa used to say: "Let us never forget the heritage which our saintly founders have left us, the heritage of humility and poverty of spirit which was the basis of all their strivings for the possession of eternal happiness. . . . If we say, as we do, that such is the basis of the restoration of our order to its primitive holiness, let us never fail to make our lives consistent with theirs."[9] Farther on she explains the reason for not advancing quickly along the road to perfection: "If anyone thinks the rule particularly difficult to accept, it is because she fundamentally lacks the true spirit of her order. The monastery in which one dwells does not decide the severity or laxity of the rule; one who is constrained not to follow the rule, or to make excuses for so doing is guilty of lack of conformity to the rule. If such a one thinks that a transfer to another monastery will be the means of saving her soul and overcoming this tepidity, she is guilty of self-deception. No-one will ever save her soul by following the way of her own spirit."[10]

The restoration of Carmel to its primitive observance was always dear to the heart of St. Theresa and she was firmly convinced that once this was achieved the order would bring special honor to the Queen of Heaven and the patroness of Carmel. This point she firmly stressed when writing to one of the first convents of the reform: "May all honor and praise be to God through the intercession of His beloved Mother, whose habit we are indeed privileged to wear." Later on she continues: "God, indeed, seems pleased with the honor and respect we accord to His Mother. For this purpose He allowed me a vision of our Lady in exceeding glory. She was wearing a white mantle with which she seemed to cover all members of the order of Carmel."[11] As if this were not enough, later on our Lord Himself reassured her of the special favor with which He regarded this order dedicated to His Blessed Mother: "Even during your lifetime you will witness the progress of this order so revered by My Mother. All her members are in a most special way dedicated to her, which imposes on them the obligation of living as her faithful children."[12]

The honor and security of each religious consists mainly in the individual's striving to bring his emotions and actions into harmony with the spirit and teachings of the saint to whose institute he has freely consecrated himself. It is a sure sign that one is in danger of losing his vocation if he feels little or no appreciation for the teachings of the saints who either founded or reformed his order. Every religious at frequent intervals should ask himself if he habitually exerts himself to act in accordance with the dictates of his conscience in acquiring and practicing the virtues inculcated into the spirit of the order by its saintly founders. Good example does not consist in words alone but in the fulfillment of what one has vowed and promised. It is not sufficient to merely say "Thy will be done" if habitually one is seeking to do not the will of God but his own will. Now it is the will of God for each religious that he keeps the vows he has promised to Him freely and of his own choice. It follows, then, that one who has promised poverty must be poor in spirit and not seek any of the exterior or interior riches of the world or he becomes guilty of scandal. This complete renunciation is internal whereby the religious seeks always only the things that are pleasing to God.

Carmelites have for their model not only the outstanding mistress of the spiritual life, St. Theresa, but the incomparable mystical writer and eloquent eulogist of God's love for souls, St. John of the Cross. It would be difficult to find a keener observer or a better analyst of the weaknesses and potentialities of men than this great saint. From the summit of his symbolic Carmel this great psychologist and master of mystics teaches and guides all who aspire to the heights of perfection, but most particularly those who are his sons and daughters because of the religious habit they wear. Yet the wearing of this religious habit can never be for anyone the claim to the true title of glory. It is a fundamental truth that the habit neither sanctifies nor saves but merely binds. It is indeed a great honor to be invested with the habit of our Lady but to do so imposes serious and lasting obligations. Every Carmelite may well glory in calling St. John of the Cross his Father and Master, but if his conscience tells him that he is far from following the true spirit of the order he will not know true peace since ". . . he who does good is of God; he who does evil has not seen God."[13]

It is well to spend some time reflecting on the obligations which we have undertaken to determine the reality of our spiritual condition and to see how closely we reflect the spirit and teachings of St. John of the Cross. We would soon become saints if we seriously and honestly reflected on points similar to the following: "Am I a true Carmelite? Do I strive to live both in private and in public accordance with the evangelical perfections recommended by the masters of perfection? How is the spirit of St. John of the Cross reflected in the actions of my daily living? If at this moment I were called to give an account of my life to God, would I in all justice feel qualified to call upon St. John of the Cross to intercede for me because of my fidelity and imitation of his virtues. . . ?"

If these questions fill us with uneasiness, then this is a well founded and salutary fear revealing the knowledge that we are not striving for perfection. With this knowledge comes the realization that the sufferings of this life are a necessity as well as a means of obtaining sanctity and that they are to be preferred to living a life of self-deception and pretense. What a disappointment life would hold at its final hour if we were to find that we have labored but in vain; that the works we had performed were of no avail in the eyes of God because they had been filled with self-seeking rather than the search for the all-loving God! Little wonder then that St. John should say: "What profit is there in giving to God that which we wish to do? We thus have received our reward! Rather let us consider what it is that God truly wishes from us at that moment and then do it. In so doing you will most assuredly obtain greater pleasure and merit than in following the dictates of your own will."[14]

God dispenses His graces to whom and in what measure He chooses, exacting from each in proportion to what He has given. At the same time, however, the religious profession places on us the obligation of making sanctity and perfection the chief goals of our lives. We are free to accept the religious life or not, but once we have accepted it we are certainly not free to alter, or to attempt to alter the divine will of God, according to our own whims and impulses. All our efforts, then, must be directed toward the acquisition of the spirit of our order, which spirit is to be found in the teaching and writings of our holy founders. For all religious, Carmelites or not, St. John of the Cross is the admirable model, inspired by God to show the paths which must be climbed to reach the summit of perfection. Of him God says to each of us, just as He said to Moses on the Mount, "Look and make according to the example that was shown thee on the Mount."[15] In the office of St. John, the Church gives us the inspiring words of the prophet Isaias, "You who seek justice and union with God, listen to the hymns of praise which have been sung by those who have gone before: Fix your eyes on Abraham, your father, and on Sara, who gives us light, because Him alone do I call and Him alone do I bless."[16]

The divine invitation is extended then to all to take as our model, St. John of the Cross. The legitimate excuse could be offered that it is difficult to follow him because of the fact that many of his works are incomprehensible as is true of those works dedicated to souls already closely united with God. But the "Counsels" are within the grasp of all who truly wish to love God and Him alone. Once they are understood the revelation is made that God is impatient to communicate Himself to certain souls, not wishing to wait until eternity to disclose to them the secrets of His heart, and so it is through the medium of such works as the "Counsels" that souls are enlightened as to the surest and quickest way of obtaining this divine union. Although it is true that many may never ascend to the heights described by St. John, yet everyone has the sacred obligation of studying and putting into practice the austere and vigorous Carmelite asceticism which was characteristic of our holy father and which has been the means of many of its members obtaining salvation.

St. John's "Counsels" enchant some as much as his famous works, *The Ascent of Mount Carmel* and *The Dark Night of the Soul*. If a religious cannot attain to the lofty mysticism contained in either of these books, he will surely find the realization of his desires in the "Counsels" since they contain all that a soul consecrated to God needs to know and to practice to reach the highest perfection. Here we find a vigorous asceticism supplemented by a lofty mysticism "The Whole is the explanation of the Nothing." In itself this may seem a contradiction: if you wish to possess "all," desire "nothing." In reality it is one of those paradoxes with which Christianity abounds. "He who freely parts with his life for My sake will win it in the end."[17]

Reflection on these words shows the reasonableness and logic of St. John's teachings. God is the ALL; to possess him fully, to the measure of our capacity, is to possess ALL; nothing is lacking to us. But to attain this end we must first empty ourselves of everything else. How can the ALL fill the soul already crowded with creatures? The demands of St. John of the Cross, then, express the exigencies of divine love which is based on self-renunciation. The entire process of ascending the Mount Carmel of St. John reduces itself to the maxim of St. Augustine: "the love of God to the contempt of self; or the love of self to the contempt of God." The choice is ours to make but only the road of "nothingness" will lead to the complete possession of "All" because what counts most "is faith that expresses itself in love."[18]

CHAPTER TWO

THE ADMONITIONS OF
ST. JOHN OF THE CROSS

Explained by St. John in his brief and admirable preface to the "Cautelas" is the highest perfection which religious can attain by faithfully observing these precautions, the facility with which this perfection may be acquired, and the intense joy which follows upon its achievement.

"The religious who desires to achieve recollection, spiritual silence, and poverty of spirit whereby he will attain union with God must practise the following instructions if he wishes to be freed from the wiles and illusions of Satan. If he carefully observes these obligations, he will rapidly advance in perfection and attain great peace of soul. Every evil to which the soul is subjected comes from one of these three sources: the world, the flesh, and the devil. The world is difficult to overcome; the devil is more difficult; but the flesh is the most difficult of all to master. In order to conquer one of these enemies it is necessary to conquer all three. With such a conquest the soul is at peace."[1]

These admonitions contain nine counsels comprising a complete treatise on religious perfection. St. John states: "He who observes these counsels with ordinary attention, without failing in the obligations imposed on him by his state of life, will rapidly advance to great perfection and obtain great peace of soul."[2]

Before studying each counsel separately we deem it prudent to consider them collectively in order to understand clearly the three enemies of man and their relation to his spiritual life.

Words are a God-given means of purifying and sanctifying ourselves in the communication of truth, light, and love. Yet, as we well know, the repetition of words causes them to lose their original force and meaning. Such a matter of routine renders words inefficacious just as routine is the deadly enemy of spiritual discipline

8

and perfection. So, too, the connotation of the words "the world, the flesh, and the devil." They have been so often repeated that they have lost their original meaning. Let us now study these words as they are understood by St. John and see how he relates them to the most vulnerable traits of our characters.

By the "world" is not meant an acceptance of any evil, because the saint presupposes that those living a religious life constantly avoid anything which is directly opposed to virtue. What he does mean by the "world" is any person, place, or thing which is an impediment to our complete union with God. Such an inordinate attachment, while not in itself sinful, deters the soul on its road to union with God. A second obstacle is an excessive desire for worldly goods. Third, there is an imprudent solicitude which causes us to interfere with domestic affairs over which we have no jurisdiction. These three precautions, then, are directed against any disorderly affection for a person, an excessive desire for temporal goods, and an imprudent zeal in worldly affairs. These are summarized by the saint as follows:

"Do not love any one person to the exclusion of another because we do not know who is truly worthy of our love. . . . Love all men alike and place your greatest affection in God.

"Do not be solicitous for any created object. Seek the kingdom of God and all these things will be given to you.

"Never repeat what you may hear of community news or of an individual religious without good reason. Even though you lived among angels you are still capable of misinterpreting the motives which prompt such words or actions."[3]

The devil is another agent who, whether we like to admit it or not, must be treated as any human being. It is true that he can have no power over us unless we permit him but he can and does subtly interfere in our intimate affairs and personal emotions. No created being can force us against our will but the evil spirit possesses a tremendous power which can cause innumerable evils unless we vigilantly watch and pray.

The vitality of a community consists in the mutual harmony of its members working in collaboration with one another. Therefore, for an individual to act in a singular manner is to detract from the greater good of the community. Although such a personal act may seem less glorious to the individual it is more efficacious to the community. In the depths of our souls we carry the germ of pride inherited from our first parents. Unconsciously this pride urges us to act singularly and these actions become one of the greatest enemies to personal perfection. Such individual acts direct their glory toward themselves and not toward God. The devil is well aware of this weakness of human nature and he exploits it to the greatest advantage by fomenting a dangerous sensitivity within us. He subtly suggests that by following our own personal inclinations we can do more good than by following the express commands of a superior. Then, too, he reasons, the superior is not prudent in his judgments and does not wish to justify the innate talents which we think we possess. St. John warns us that such diabolical interference is very difficult to detect because the susceptibilities of self-love are so deeply rooted in our being. To overcome such diabolical intrusions he suggests:

> Never perform any action, no matter how good and charitable it may seem, except under obedience. Any action which is not regulated by obedience is worthless.
> Never look upon your superior, whoever he may be, except as a representative of God. . . . Many religious fail in their vocation by not regarding their superiors as those appointed by God.
> Strive with all your heart to attain humility in thought, word and deed, wishing sincerely that others be preferred to you in all things.[4]

In addition to the pleasures of the world and the suggestions of the devil, we must also be careful to regulate any irregular desires which may arise. Human nature, weakened by the sin of our first parents and impoverished by personal transgressions, requires constant self-disciplining. No matter how dear a sick man may be to us personally, we do not hesitate to deny him many things which he may ardently desire, because we know that such things are dangerous to his well-being. All human beings are more or less morally sick and therefore suffer hallucinations which can be reduced to two principal ones.

First, we tend to make ourselves the center of our little world around which pivots all those with whom we are in close association. If this natural inclination is not prudently and energetically restrained it will prove a prolific source of innumerable grievances and sufferings.

This selfishness causes an aversion for all who do not think or act as we do. This aversion varies from the first almost imperceptible movement of a contradiction of a dear friend to violent hatred of a powerful enemy. So many and varied are these aversions that it is impossible to classify them according to number or kind. Against such destructive hallucinations, which prove the enemy of peace, justice, and charity St. John offers admirable advice: "The main purpose of your being in a monastery is to become the servant of all. . . . Superiors have been placed over us to admonish us and to aid us in overcoming self. . . ."[5]

A second hallucination from which we unconsciously suffer is the pleasure we derive from the actions we perform, as if they were the end and not the means to the end. In this, we mistake the pleasure for the obligation. We cannot deny that we are punctual in performing the actions we naturally like, while on the other hand we are reluctant to do and perhaps omit entirely the lesser obligations which seem displeasing to us.

To remedy this evil inclination St. John proposes the following two admonitions which are severely ascetical, so much so that exact observance of them would suffice to make us great saints.

"Never omit anything which may cause a natural repugnance. Never perform any action for the sole pleasure which may be derived from this action, even if it is directed toward God. The truly spiritual man seeks in his actions what is unpleasant and disagreeable to his nature; otherwise he will not destroy self love nor acquire the love of God."[6]

In his famous "Cautelas" St. John intended to lead his sons and daughters to the highest perfection in the simplest manner possible. Since the saint directs his admonitions to the interior man, he asks a strict discipline of spirit which is not contrary to reason nor fulfillment; nothing is proposed which cannot be realized by any person desiring to lead an interior life. There is no question of long penances, of many readings, nor of long hours of meditation. Rather the saint limits himself to regulating affections and possession of temporal goods which he generically terms the "world," as well as guarding against the deceits of the devil and the subtle insinuations of self-love which he calls the "flesh."

When these three enemies, the world, the flesh, and the devil, are conquered there are no other enemies left to fight since the soul is raised to a height beyond the grasp of material objects, now enjoying the consolations of the Holy Spirit.

This frees the soul so it can advance rapidly on its ascent to Mt. Carmel. Here we must travel the road of blind faith until we finally attain the goal, God. Faith is the "midnight" and God is the "Coming Day."[7] Such a faith is possible only to those who have striven to overcome the world, the flesh, and the devil, since God is not accessible to either the understanding or the senses. It is this blind faith which must progressively divest man of all that is not God because "Narrow is the gate and straight the way that leads to life . . . and few there are that find it."[8]

CHAPTER THREE

THE FIRST ADMONITION AGAINST THE WORLD

Before beginning a commentary on the first precaution it seems proper to reproduce the text.

> To escape from the dangers of the world three things must be observed. One must show an equal love and disinterestedness in all men, whether they be relatives or not. Such mortification of natural affection is necessary to acquire spiritual perfection. Obligations toward one's relatives can be better discharged when performed through the motive of love of God.
>
> Do not love any person more than another, otherwise such affections may become inordinate. Do not think about them, neither good nor evil. . . . Avoid them as much as possible, otherwise it will be difficult to obtain perfection.
>
> If you take liberties, allowing your affections free license, Satan will soon deceive you or you will deceive yourself under the pretence of good and evil.
>
> Only by following these admonitions can you expect to be freed from inordinate affections which deter the soul from giving itself completely to God.[1]

To many people the teachings contained in these precautions may seem extremely severe:

> Detach yourself completely from your relatives and friends, but most particularly from your relatives. . . . Regard each human being as a stranger, not loving one in preference to the other. . . . Do not think about them neither good nor evil. If you fail to observe this you will never become a true religious. . . .[2]

Taken literally and without explanation these words are subject to misunderstanding. A highly esteemed religious was asked how he interpreted this passage and he candidly remarked: "Several sincere persons have asked me the same question and I must admit I do not know how to answer them. To my way of thinking these words are written for novices only, because I do not see how they can otherwise be faithfully observed."[3]

This is a lamentable error. Although St. John wrote these admonitions specifically for the novices of his order, their message was not meant to be transitory.

These counsels are directed toward the formation of the interior man and his conscience as a means of strengthening his character, so each man will be able to adapt himself to the varied circumstances of his environment but never to the detriment of his ultimate union with God. A religious should be the most flexible of men readily adapting himself to all situations; yet, so completely immersed in the love of God that he can say with St. Paul: "I became all things to all men to gain all. . . ."[4]

St. John of the Cross, a man of practical talent and holiness, was also endowed with the gifts of a perfect educator. Since his aim was to form this interior man in his disciples so strongly that no created object could interfere, it is also evident that he did not train his novices simply for the period of their novitiate but for their entire religious life. Neither did he intend to keep these instructions simply for his own followers; rather he wished that they be transmitted to all those desiring to acquire religious perfection.

The mind of an author cannot be judged by a few passages he may have written no matter how decisive these works may be. One must seek deep into the work in order to determine the true message the author wished to convey. If the author is a saint and treating of spiritual matters, his actions should be considered as a reflection of his inner life. Consequently, if it can be proved that St. John was not cold and indifferent in his dealing with others, then we can also conclude that he did not demand absolute forgetfulness nor absolute indifference, as such, from those who would strive for perfection. Fortunately, St. John, though a great lover of solitude, still maintained a communication with the outer world. As the reformer of his order and the founder of a number of convents and monasteries, as well as the director of countless souls, we can determine the depth of his character and his nobility of soul. Due to these relations, we can conclude that he was sensible, solicitous, affectionate, and paternal.

The private and confidential letters of an author reflect his soul better than all his works put together. Due to the number of persons whom he influenced, the correspondence of St. John is extensive. Unfortunately many of his doctrinal and literary epistles were destroyed when dissension was directed against him. Divine Providence, however, did not permit all of this correspondence to be destroyed because some of his entire letters as well as fragments have been collected by his loving disciples. These provide a means of contemplating the saint as he actually was and reveal the true grandeur of his heart.

Interpreting his first admonition literally the letters of St. John should be strictly business, concise and dictatorial, revealing the saint as entirely oblivious of the human nature of his correspondent. This is anything but true. In a letter to a nun he laments bitterly, though with resignation, that from the time of his imprisonment he had not seen St. Theresa nor any of his religious brethren.

> Jesus be in your soul, my daughter! Though I do not know where you are, I trust that our good Mother will forward this message to you. If you are not with her, then console yourself because I am more lonely and exiled than you. Since the time of my imprisonment I have not been worthy of seeing her nor anyone else. God has done this for our good; for loneliness is a great teacher and to suffer in darkness is the way to great light.[5]

Surely this reveals one who is deeply interested in the concerns of his fellow man. A further evidence of his paternal interest in those who sought his advice is found in the following letter:

> All your letters have been received. I have shared your griefs, your trials and your desolations. They are all calling for a greater love which will inspire more fervent prayers to ascend to God so that He might grant what your soul so earnestly seeks. Thank God for the grace to pray always for His poor and neglected. . . . It would grieve me deeply to think you really believe what you wrote. . . . After your many kindnesses it would be impossible to forget you, and your intentions are always close to my heart. . . .[6]

We must bear indelibly upon our minds that the writer of these letters is the same as that of the first admonition which seems rigorous and heartless.

Yet in no way whatsoever did St. John contradict his teachings by his conduct nor did he pretend to preach to his followers what he himself did not practice. His affection for others is always concealed in his deep spirit of self-abnegation. The following is a fragment of one of his admirable letters to the sisters at Beas:

> Jesus and Mary be with you my daughters. Your letters greatly consoled me and may our Divine Lord reward you for them. Never fail, no matter what good or evil may befall you, to keep your hearts calm and filled with love for your fellow men. Perfection is so momentous that it is impossible to make progress without suffering in silence. I know from experience that the soul which is ready to converse with men is not ready to converse with God. If it were, then it would be drawn forcibly inward, loving silence and avoiding all conversation save with God. For God wants the soul to rejoice in Him rather than in any creature. . . .[7]

Such texts could be multiplied indefinitely portraying the real understanding of the doctrine contained in the first admonition. It is not among the saints, and particularly among the followers of St. John, that one can find persons who are incapable of love and solicitude for their neighbors. Their personal lives may have been spent in solitude, completely isolated from the world, alone in the universe that surrounded them, yet this being alone with the great Alone did not render them incapable of feeling emotions other than their own. Those who do not know the greatness of love shared with others love but themselves, and surely such lovers of self cannot be placed among the disciples of St. John any more than they can be reckoned as true followers of Christ.

The Divine Master also exacted a great price from His disciples. In His own words: ". . . He who loves father or mother more than Me is not worthy of Me. . . . If you do not hate your father and mother, wife, and brother for my sake, and even your own life, you cannot be my disciple. . . ."[8] Who would dare to say that by these words Christ wished to destroy or minimize the holy affections and love which He Himself placed in the human heart? The same Master, who said these words, inspired the greatest love of His disciples so that later they could write thus:

> Everyone who loves is born of God and knows God. He who does not love, does not know God. . . .[9] He who loves his brother abides in the light. . . . He who hates his brother is in darkness, and he does not know whither he goes, because the darkness has blinded his eyes. . . .[10]

The same Savior who utters such apparently severe words teaches us on other occasions the greatness of the love of the human heart. Did He not love His Immaculate Mother with a tenderness no son has ever shown to his mother? Did He not shed tears of sympathy at the intense grief of Mary at the tomb of her beloved brother? On the night of the Last Supper did He not speak to the humble fishermen with the greatest of tenderness and with a love yet unknown to men, even permitting one of them to rest his head upon His divine Heart? If the adorable heart of the God-Man reacted so magnificently to the sensibilities of the human heart, it is impossible to believe that He intended to destroy in our hearts any affection which had for its immediate end the love of God, even though a cursory reading may give this impression. It is impossible that God can be contradictory in His words or actions.

The magnificent love of God has chosen creatures to be the object of His predilection, not with an exclusive love but with a love which surpasses all human loves, a paradoxical love, which intensely loves the individual while simultaneously embracing all men; a love which is not simply limitless but rather inexhaustible and ever increasing, directing all human affections back to the source from which they came, namely God. So marvelous was this love that Christ did not come to extinguish this mutual and reciprocal love found among men but rather to purify it so all men might come to love their neighbor in the heart of God. In a most solemn moment the divine Master proclaimed love the fulfilling of the law, the synthesis of all the obligations of men. "A new commandment I give unto you: that you love one another as I have loved you."[11]

The entire doctrine on love, as given by St. John, can be reduced to three points:

1. No work, no matter how well accomplished it may be, is worthy of God if it is not permeated with charity.
2. No human love is acceptable to God, if it does not accord with the love God has for each of His creatures. "I have given you an example, that as I have done, so you do also."[12]
3. The perfection of love consists in the fact that we love all men equally, in God and for God, showing to each the same love which God reserves for privileged souls.

Viewing the admonitions of St. John from this point we find that his teachings are in complete accord with the teachings of Christ. He asks no sacrifice other than that asked by Christ Himself.

Rather he teaches that we must love our fellow man as Christ has loved us. We know well that Christ loved men infinitely and because of this love He readily sympathized with them in all their trials and sorrows ever showing them the greatest of affection and love. Yet He loved His eternal Father more, even to the extent of not hesitating to separate Himself from the love of His creatures when the glory of His Father required it. The love of Christ for His Mother was incomparable, yet He did not hesitate to sacrifice His blood for all men even though this sacrifice of His life meant the breaking of His Mother's heart. With this double sacrifice of the Son and His Mother, Divine Providence was pleased to redeem the world. From the price demanded for the Redemption we can conclude that the moral world rests on the double column of love and sacrifice. No human act can be worthy of God unless it is accompanied by sacrifice; no sacrifice can be accepted by God unless it is the result of a free and generous love of man.

That which is most important is often most difficult to understand. Thus it is difficult to reason why the heart may love intensely yet leave the will perfectly free to follow the dictates of the conscience and the inspirations of God. The entire moral life of man consists in a correct understanding of this truth. Even St. John admits the difficulty of maintaining freedom of spirit while loving intensely as the following paragraph shows:

> The more material objects I love, the more involved I become, because the object loved and the lover become identified as one . . . so much so that I can no more disregard this object than I can forget my own soul, because I live more in the object of my love than I do in myself.[13]

Complete detachment from created objects consists in an interior renunciation, while exteriorly the creature is esteemed and reverenced, not for what he is in himself but what he is because of his God-given talents. In other words, one loves God in his neighbor and the more intensely one loves God, the more he will love his neighbor.

The beautiful soul of St. John is reflected in his deep love of the cross, his solitude and retirement. Nevertheless he always manifested the greatest charity toward those who sought his guidance. By so doing the saint was not contradicting his admonition: "Do not love one in preference to another . . . treat all as strangers . . ." because grace does not destroy but rather elevates human nature. A letter written to St. Theresa offers ample proof of the type of charity demanded by St. John:

> When my relatives and friends come to me asking advice and seeking consolation, I ought not to treat them as if they were not bodily present, or as if their problems were of no concern of mine. To divest ourselves of earthly affections does not mean a lack of concern. Rather as Christ Himself says: Know ye that the law in itself is valueless if it is not subordinated to charity. The letter of the law killeth but the spirit quickeneth.[14]. . . When souls sick with suffering and discouragement come to me, my love for them, displayed in my words and deeds of encouragement, should help to lighten their burden. Likewise everything possible should be done to alleviate their sufferings.[15]

From this beautiful passage it is clear that neither in the name of virtue nor the laws of the constitution is affection for one's relatives or friends forbidden. Love of neighbor is most praiseworthy; what is to be condemned is disorderly affection. Natural love must be completely subordinated to supernatural charity, which renunciation purifies the soul, bringing it to a higher and more perfect love.

CHAPTER FOUR

OUR NEIGHBOR

Contrary to the impressions derived from a casual reading of the first of his admonitions, St. John of the Cross condemns neither the pure and orderly love of man nor of creatures. Rather he wishes to direct and sanctify such affections so that they will be a foretaste of the friendships of heaven. True followers of God will find in this austere monk the best apostle and eulogist of genuine love. His poetic and saintly soul considered all creatures as a reflection of the love of God and he exhorts the tiniest work of creation to remind him of this love: "If you shall see Him Whom I love, tell Him, I languish, suffer and die in search of my love. I will go over mountains and strands, nor will I have other employment, My sole occupation is love."[1]

According to St. John of the Cross, life is of value only in so far as it teaches, tests, and purifies our love. With each new degree of love there is new joy. This idea of love is developed in an entire book of St. John called the "Spiritual Canticle" from which this famous quotation is taken: "In the eventide of your life you will be examined as to your love. . . ." St. John knows that God is incomprehensible and yet everything speaks to him of God as his works show. Notice the beauty and love described in this excerpt from the "Spiritual Canticle":

> My Beloved is in the mountains,
> The solitary wooded valleys
> The strange islands, the roaring torrents
> The whisper of the amorous gales;
> The tranquil night;
> At the approaches of the dawn,
> The silent music, the murmuring solitude
> The eventide which revives, and enkindles love.

Thus the retirement from the world so highly recommended by St. John is not a smothering or elimination of emotions; on the contrary, it is the means of purifying them so they will "burn the more in love."[2] The soul then becomes completely cauterized and turned into one wound of love; yet it is precisely healthy, because it is so wounded.

Frigid souls which will not react to love are not the souls spoken of by St. John. Sweetness of spirit and tenderness of soul are the effects of God's love; callousness and frigidity are the fruit of pride. "The soul filled with love is meek, gentle, humble, and patient while the soul that does not love is hard and brittle because of its own selfishness."[3]

If anyone wishes to interpret these words as referring only to the love of God and not his neighbor, let him consider the well-known words of Scripture: "If any man say, I love God and hateth his brother; he is a liar. For he that loveth not his brother whom he seeth, how can he love God, whom he seeth not?"[4]

Throughout the works of St. John we find some decisive statements relative to this matter. The Saint, a learned theologian and deep observer of the human heart, preaches a love of God supplemented by love of neighbor. He emphasizes that these two loves, the human and the divine, complement one another; they grow and bear fruit in perfection. As St. Paul says, "Love beareth all things, hopeth all things, endureth all things."[5] The actual words of St. John of the Cross relative to love of neighbor are: "When the love we have for creatures is purely spiritual then the love of God grows proportionately. The more we remember the earthly love the more we remember God and desire Him. If this love springs from a purely natural or sensual inclination the more one thinks of that affection, the more he withdraws from God and he is filled with remorse of conscience. Thus love which is born of sensuality ends in sensuality; that which is born of God, ends in God. This is the difference between these two loves so that man may distinguish between them."[6]

St. John of the Cross, then, is not the enemy of love. He wishes the heart to be purified so it can contain a greater love; so it may be capable of loving not only God, but loving all in God and for God, whatever according to Him is just and lovable. Thus it is not strange to hear him say, "All our good works, then, must have their origin in God if they are to be pure and holy. . . . The soul that loves is neither wearied nor wearies, for he who knows how to die to all, will find life in all."[7]

The spiritual advancement of a soul is like the flight of an eagle; the higher it soars, the greater the freedom with which it flies and the keener is its sight. When selfishness or natural sympathy motivates our love it becomes narrow and limited. Such a soul is completely absorbed with self and there is no room for love of others. When a man begins to love his neighbor primarily for the love of God, then his spiritual vision increases, his heart is liberated, and the capacity for loving embraces all men. St. Theresa, speaking of such a soul, says,

> The soul, indifferent to the love of self, or of the world, becomes filled with the love of all creatures loving them only for the sake of God. Such a love of both friend and enemy would be thought incredible unless so proved by experience.[8]

The more closely a soul approaches God by its sanctity of life, the more it resembles God. Such a growth in holiness is thus described by St. John:

> The soul which labors to divest itself of all that is not God, for the sake of God, becomes enlightened and transformed, in such a manner that it seems completely possessed of God.[9]

As God loves the entire human race collectively, and yet delights in each soul individually, so the true friends of God love all mankind and each individual. The saints excluded no one from their affections, yet they did not love each with the same degree of intensity. They had a special love for those who were nearest to God, but a paternal love for those who were most in need of it, because they were the farthest away from God. In proportion to their sanctity, three characteristics predominate: A sincere, practical love for all, a predilection for those closest to God, and a paternal solicitude for those in greatest need. The divine Redeemer uses these same characteristics to draw souls to Him and then, in turn, He communicates His love to them. This form of love is predominant in the life of St. John.

The rigor of his first admonition, more ideal than real, was to prepare the soul for a more universal and solicitous charity for our neighbor. The following beautiful passage confirms and illustrates his doctrine on the advantage of detachment from creatures:

> The more a heart withdraws itself from earthly attachments, the more it prepares itself for the love of God and neighbor. When

the affections are freed from natural motives, the soul loves creatures, rationally and spiritually, as God wills them to be loved. Such a love results in liberty of spirit and a greater love of God for His own sake. The deeper our love of God becomes the more we love our neighbor for the principle of both loves is the same.[10]

St. John knew well the sensitivity of the human heart and how limited and self-centered its affections could become. He was also well aware that in the exercise of their ministry religious would be exposed to the dangers of loving creatures solely for themselves. In an effort to prevent such an evil St. John advocated that we love creatures, not for their personal attraction toward us, but solely for the love of God. The Mystical Doctor loved creatures in this manner, fully cognizant of the affections which grew out of sympathy and ties of blood. He know well the cost of ascending the heights from which one loves men as God loves them. Consequently, he warned, ". . . Consider all as strangers. . . . Do not love one person more than another for you do not know who is more worthy of love. . . ."[11]

Here, then, is the remedy against the natural defects and weaknesses of the human heart, the remedy characteristic of the educational system of St. John. Like all masters of the spiritual life, from those who limit themselves to the general practice of Christian virtues, and those who endeavor to lead souls to the highest perfection and union with God, he urges a mortification of the affections without which moral or spiritual advancement is impossible. They who do not learn to control their hearts will never learn to become saints. Against such human weakness St. John, as well as other masters of the spiritual life, proposes the remedy which will strike deep at the root of the evil. He forbids the slightest disorderly attachment which stands in the way of perfection, ". . . love not one person more than another, lest you go astray. . . ."

Every Christian must of necessity practice virtue; but God will require more of religious because He has given them more grace. A vocation to the religious life is a magnificent gift from God to which He has attached numerous graces; therefore every religious is bound, by the very nature of his calling, to strive for perfection. The teaching of St. John in regard to this is decisive, requiring a strict regulation of all human affections. There is little doubt that a religious would entertain an affection which was morally wrong, nevertheless it is well to examine oneself minutely relative to inordinate affections.

Do your affections cause you anxiety or distraction? Are you less considerate with those to whom you are not naturally attracted, perhaps being a little unjust toward them? Are there persons who make you lose time which should be employed for other matters, or prevent you from being present at community exercises? Does the attention you render to these persons render you less sincere with your Superior or with yourself? Does it cause you to violate your religious obligations, large or small? Are you becoming more sensitive toward those who do not think as you do? Upon close examination you may find that perhaps affections which at first seemed so innocent are now drawing you away from God rather than closer to Him. Perhaps you will be bound to acknowledge, too, that these affections render you lukewarm and less submissive to the divine Will, more sensitive toward those who correct you, less amiable toward your brethren, and cause more and more inobservances of the religious life. If your conscience does not answer favorably on these points, then you can be reasonably certain that such affections are inordinate and should be discontinued.

If there are sufficient reasons for continuing a friendship, then you must be prudent and regulate the attachments of your heart. It is evident that reason and charity at times require more contact with one person than with another. What St. John requires is that these friendships be regulated by prudence and charity and not merely by natural inclinations and affections. If this is so, you will never need to fear the imprecations of the saint.

Coldness toward our neighbor is never a sign of Christian virtue, much less of perfection. Indifference is a mark of hardness of heart and is the daughter of pride and selfishness. Let us constantly bear in mind that it is possible to regulate the affectionate feelings of our hearts according to God's will and to keep them alive regardless of the many vicissitudes and contradictions we shall necessarily experience in our intercourse with our neighbor. It is true that there is danger that the affectionate heart may err, but there is still greater danger that, if we are not charitable, the heart will die because of its continued coldness toward our fellow men. One of the greatest evils St. Paul noticed in human nature was the want of charity. "Foolish, dissolute, without affection, without fidelity, without mercy. . . ."[12]

God is charity and they who approach nearer to Him by holiness of life share with Him more intimately in His infinite charity, which they in turn diffuse among their neighbors. The heart which is naturally rich in affection possesses a great treasure. To become a saint it is simply necessary to regulate these affections.

One must not think that the ideal of Christian virtue consists in becoming insensible to all things. Perpetual youthfulness of heart, notwithstanding the cares and tribulations of human nature, is characteristic of the saints. Perfect Christian virtue and great religious perfection lie essentially in complete self-forgetfulness and in self-sacrifice. It comprises an abundant love of neighbor, lavishing on them great affection and many favors, expecting nothing in return, except from God. Thus the heart becomes purified more readily, pleases God more effectively, and gains more merit than from severe penances or notable acts of mortification. This is the real meaning of St. John's doctrine: "The clean of heart are called by our Divine Savior blessed, for blessedness is given to nothing less than true love."[13] This is in complete conformity with the doctrine expressed likewise by the great St. Theresa: "Happy the loving heart, which has placed its thoughts on God alone. . . . The greatest glory we can give to God consists in serving Him according to evangelical perfection . . . nothing else has value nor usefulness for man. . . ."[14]

Therefore the end which St. John has in mind is the exact fulfillment of the divine precept: "A new commandment I give to you, that you love one another, as I have loved you."[15]

This is the distinctive mark of Christ's followers: "By this shall all men know that you are my disciples, if you have love one for another."[16] "For he who loves his neighbor has fulfilled the law. Love therefore is the fulfillment of the law."[17]

When the fire of love is burning intensely in the soul, every action and every mortification acquires an infinite value. When grace and love inspire everything in our life, then it has become a perpetual hymn to the glory of God "For we are Christ's incense offered to God."[18] Love changes action into contemplation and causes contemplation to overflow into action. Love inebriates you;

love sobers you. Love makes you despise your own beauty because you are and never can be beautiful enough for Him. Love puts you at the mercy of the Beloved and emboldens you to beg for His love despite your unworthiness. Finally, love initiates you into the joy of the cross, and gives you a foretaste of eternal bliss. Thus love began by separating and ends by embracing all. It began by loving nothing but God; it ends by loving all things in God. This, then, is the real meaning of the "Counsels" of St. John of the Cross.

No matter what the literal sense of St. John's admonitions may appear, it is evident that he does not intend to restrict the love of man's heart either toward God or his fellow man. What he does intend is that the exhibition and regulation of our affections be mature and in compliance with the divine precept of perfection. His final aim is to make man's control of his emotions so holy, so sane, so forgetful of itself, and so filled with the love of God that we will love all men solely as God Himself first has loved us. In so doing the love which has drawn the Son of God down to earth will nurture and increase the love which will draw the sons of man up to heaven.

CHAPTER FIVE

MATERIAL GOODS

"The second admonition against the world relates to material goods. To free oneself of a misuse of temporal goods and to moderate a desire for them, we should be completely indifferent to, and even abhor all personal possessions. Neither should we be solicitous for what we eat, drink, or wear, but rather should we be concerned with the things of God and all these others shall be given to us. Such a spirit of indifference will cause great interior recollection and peace of soul."[1]

St. Thomas Aquinas teaches that the main object of religious life is to free us of any impediments to perfect charity. Inordinate love of material goods, as well as inordinate affections, tend to weaken this charity in our souls.[2] Therefore, with the same rigorousness that he applied to the first admonition, St. John teaches, in the second admonition, how to regulate our attachment for earthly goods. "If you earnestly desire to escape the evils attached to inordinate love of material goods, then you must hold all personal possessions in abhorrence."[3] The reason for this is admirably stated: "The incomparable gifts of God can be contained only in a heart which has been emptied of earthly attachments."[4]

In order to practice this doctrine with facility and to understand it as portrayed by St. John it is necessary to study it minutely. In itself, a certain attachment for worldly possessions is not an evil, rather it is a necessity. Almighty God, after creating man, showed him the beauties and treasures of the earth, making man the master of all: ". . . And God blessed them saying, Increase and multiply, and fill the earth, and subdue it, and rule over . . . all living creatures that move upon the earth."[5]

God, thus speaking to our first parents, gave them power over all creations, and although our power has been weakened by sin, we have still inherited the right of dominion over all created objects. The eagerness for possession, then, is natural to the human heart, and for this very reason the word *mine* has a fascination to every human being. Children pronounce the word *mine* with great pride when displaying their toys. Magnates, when referring to their industries use this word with great arrogance. If this word thus awakens such a response in both old and young it is because the idea it expresses is innate and a natural aspiration of the human soul. Consequently the desire for material goods is not to be condemned, not even in the name of mysticism, for one truth cannot be at variance with another. God has not filled the human heart with an infinite capacity for possession unless He meant this desire to be filled. Neither has He made such a magnificent creature simply for us to ignore it or despise it, nor has He given us the power to dominate and possess the things of creation simply to disregard them. Rather what God demands of us is to discipline and moderate the desires for material blessings.

St. John recommends detachment so strongly, simply because he wishes us to possess all things in God. It is evident from the following beautiful passage that St. John understands well the real meaning of the word *mine*:

> Thou wilt not take away from me, my God, what thou hast given me, through the merits of Thy beloved Son. Mine are the heavens; mine is the earth, mine are the just; mine are all sinners; mine are the angels and the Mother of God. All things are mine. God Himself is mine and exists for me, for Christ is mine, and all for me. What then dost thou desire and ask for, my soul? All this is thine, and all is for thee. Do not be satisfied with the crumbs which fall from Thy Father's table but rather exult and glory in the greatness of His creation and you shall obtain the desires of your heart.[6]

The inclination to possess and to dominate all earthly goods which God has so lavishly bestowed on all mankind corresponds to the command given to our first parents: "Fill the earth, and subdue it."[7] These are the words of God; therefore the desire for possessions cannot in itself be wrong. Before pronouncing this command God prepared the heart of man with the necessary disposition for receiving such a gift, filling man's heart with desires as ardent and imperishable as human nature itself.

Man cannot destroy anything which is a part of his nature without at the same time destroying himself, but he can and often does weaken and profane the gifts of God, causing the noblest aspirations of his spirit to deviate from their proper object. This, man has done relative to his desire for possessions, unfortunately making his material goods a prolific source of disorder. Through an inordinate love for earthly possessions man has been guilty of injustice to his fellow men by depriving them of their right to a proportionate share for the same goods. He has showed himself ungrateful to God by giving to creatures the love which is due to the Creator for there is no room in the heart filled with creature love for the all-possessing love of God. How familiar man is with the axiom that God is a jealous God. Thus instead of using these gifts for the service of God and his neighbor, pride converts them into an idol which is an insult to God.

Every natural aspiration of the human spirit is indestructible because it flows immediately from human nature and mediately from God, the Author of nature. Therefore this aspiration cannot be destroyed but rather must be educated and controlled. Without this control the desire for temporal goods, which in itself is good and holy, will become an inexhaustible source of evil which leads theologians to place covetousness among the capital sins. The poor maid who in her daily marketing discounts a few cents; the merchant who deceives his customer; the usurer who pitilessly ruins his unfortunate victim; the potentate who reduces to misery a multitude of small businessmen to add millions to his own; the timid nun who conceals something of trivial value; the priest who scandalizes his people by the manner in which he exacts the offering that is due to the church; the religious who in the management of community or personal affairs breaks one of the fundamental vows of religious life; each, in his own way, is guilty of covetousness. Were it not for an unbridled desire of possessing, great crimes would be avoided in the world and a multiplicity of disturbances in religious life would never be realized.

Our divine Lord came to heal this evil deeply rooted in the human heart. To the great surprise of those who did not understand His spirit of poverty, the Savior showed Himself as one enamored of poverty of spirit, extolling it by His example and doctrine. He was born poor, He lived in complete poverty, He was always surrounded by the poor, and finally He died an outcast of society. As if His own example were not sufficient He eulogized poverty in His preaching, denouncing those who were inordinately attached to riches. With an indignation never before witnessed in His demeanor He drove the buyers and sellers out of the temple. The fearful imprecations: "Woe to you who are rich: for you have your consolation!"[8] as well as "I say to you: it is easier for a camel to pass through the eye of a needle, than for a rich man to enter into the kingdom of heaven,"[9] are directed toward an inordinate love of created objects.

On the other hand He began His sermon on the Mount with sublime praise for the poor and humble: "Blessed are the poor in spirit for theirs is the kingdom of heaven. Blessed are the meek. . . . Blessed are the clean of heart. . . ."[10]

Thus Christ identified Himself with the poor, promising to recompense every deed done to them as done to Himself.

To remove from human hearts all superfluous affection for worldly goods He addressed these familiar and charming discourses to His disciples, a few poor men whom He commissioned to reform the world: "Behold the birds of the air, for they neither sow, nor do they reap, nor gather into barns; and your heavenly Father feeds them. Are you not of much more value than they? . . . Consider the lilies of the field, how they grow; they labor not, neither do they spin. But I say to you that not even Solomon in all his glory was arrayed as one of these. And if the grass of the field, which is today and tomorrow is cast into the oven, God doth so clothe; how much more you, O ye of little faith? . . . For your Father knoweth that you have need of all these things. Seek ye therefore first the kingdom of God and all these things shall be added unto you."[11]

As if this were still not enough to detach the human heart, He enriched His teachings with magnificent promises for those who would renounce worldly goods for His sake. They would receive a hundredfold in this life for the renunciation which would make such souls His assessors on Judgment Day. Realizing these admonitions and promises it is not surprising that generous souls have willingly renounced material goods. Never has there been a saint who was not poor in spirit. We, who are striving for religious perfection, have likewise solemnly promised to abandon the goods of the earth in order to imitate Christ, for the vow of poverty is one of the essential conditions of religious life. Furthermore, it is impossible for a religious order to prosper without the spirit of poverty.

Religious orders, however, are not composed of angels but of human beings confronted with a multiplicity of material needs for their well-being. Since we cannot reasonably expect Divine Providence to fulfill these needs miraculously it is evident that religious orders are not forbidden to possess earthly goods. God blesses holy poverty, but never misery. It may be true that riches are a danger to virtue, but it is likewise true that it is impossible to preserve peace in a community where the necessities of life are lacking. This interpretation of poverty is in accord with the doctrine of St. John, who says that poverty is not to be *in want* of necessities, but *in detachment* from these things.

For this purpose we have the vow and the virtue of holy poverty. The vow is negative and the virtue is positive. The vow teaches us what must be avoided in the line of material goods, so the principle of religious life is not destroyed. The virtue teaches us how to use these objects according to the spirit of Christ. As a general rule religious do not sin gravely against the vow of poverty. Yet the propensity to appropriate material goods may often blind his conscience to a nonobservance of the spirit of poverty.

It was the intention of St. John in this admonition to instruct us in the practice of the virtue of poverty toward which the vow tends, since he presupposed that his followers are sufficiently instructed in transgressions against the vow of poverty. The vow is the means, the virtue the end; and since the means are useless unless directed toward the end, the vow is meaningless if it does not train us to acquire the true spirit of poverty recommended by Christ to all who would become saints. St. Thomas Aquinas, as well as St. Augustine and St. Jerome, define the true poverty of spirit as an interior renunciation of temporal objects, which renunciation includes a motivation by the Holy Ghost and an annihilation of the spirit of pride. Consequently poverty of spirit does not consist in the renunciation of exterior goods; rather it abides in the soul. Since this renunciation is motivated by the Holy Ghost it becomes a supernatural virtue, directly opposed to the conceit and pride caused by disorderly affection for material goods.

It is clear that one may legally possess and manage material goods without being inordinately attached to them. St. Ferdinand, St. Louis, and David were not materially poor, yet despite their riches they were poor in spirit, otherwise they would not have been saints.

The vow of poverty is a most efficacious means of obtaining poverty of spirit. This disqualifies a religious from legally possessing anything of his own. This also pertains to personal administration of, as well as the disposal of any property which may be inherited by or willed to an individual religious after his profession of the vow. Yet it is possible that a religious who has never broken the vow of poverty is not really poor in spirit. This is true if he harbors any attachment for created objects, for material objects can never fully satisfy the soul. The saint, as an experienced master, recommends extreme vigilance in the management of temporal goods, since selfishness can very easily blind us to our actual motives. Only by humble prayer and frequent and careful examination of conscience can we know what spirit is actually prompting us. If pride has disappeared and we allow ourselves to be deprived of little things with peace and resignation, if we accept the thousand small privations and contradictions met with in religious life, then we can conclude that we are being motivated by the Holy Ghost, since the proper effect of the spirit of poverty is the destruction of pride and vanity.

If, after years in the religious life, we still are lacking the spirit of poverty, we have defeated the main purpose of the vow. Our divine Redeemer desired that religious, as followers of His spirit of poverty, should be a constant contradiction to the covetousness so deeply rooted in humanity. If, then, there is no greater spirit of poverty to be noticed among religious than among seculars, there is reason for great concern. It is not the value of the article which is important but rather the loss of purity and liberty of spirit which the Lord seeks in His beloved poor. This is what St. John means when he says: ". . . the soul held by bonds of human affections, however slight they may be, cannot make its way to God. . . ."[12]

Nonobservance of this teaching has been the cause of ruin to many souls. Such souls believe that since their conscience does not bother them concerning the vow of poverty they are fulfilling the spirit of poverty. This is far from the truth, because excessive attachment to a book, habit, room, or place is not poverty of spirit, neither does it bring upon the religious the blessing of God. This is verified by St. John:

God is justly angry with certain souls whom He has called to Himself and to perfection. Yet these very souls are weak and unmortified, not caring to surrender all to God, Who, therefore, permits them to become less and less perfect.[13]

A single restless and unmortified soul brings more injury to the community than many wicked demons. Scripture tells us that only one among the faithful was guilty of breaking the law of God yet God did not bless nor protect the group until the culprit was removed and punished. Again at the Last Supper the presence of the avaricious Judas caused a restraint among the Apostles which was immediately removed when Judas withdrew. Thus a single unmortified soul disturbs the peace of an entire community and prevents the presence of Christ among them. On the other hand, the exact observance of this admonition will be the basis of a perpetual source of spiritual and material blessings. The admonition of St. John of the Cross relative to material goods can be summed up in the following:

Keep the spirit of poverty and have a contempt for earthly possessions, desiring to content yourself with God alone. Understand well that you be conscious of no necessities other than those to which you wish to subject your hearts; for he who is poor in spirit is constant and joyful in privation, since he has made nothing and nothingness his all. Blessed is that nothingness and blessed is that secret place in his heart that possesses everything because it possesses nothing for itself, but casts away all care so that it may concentrate more fully on the love of God.[14]

CHAPTER SIX

THE THIRD ADMONITION
AGAINST THE WORLD

The third admonition is directed toward our relations with the fellow members of the religious order to which we belong. Non-observance of this admonition leads to the loss of peace of soul and may well be the cause of sin. The admonition of St. John reads thus:

> Do not be concerned with any one religious in particular. Never let your mind dwell on him, nor on his actions, nor speak about his faults except to proper authority. Neither marvel at nor be scandalized at what you may see or hear, keeping your soul in complete oblivion of all around you. Even if you lived among angels you would not be able to understand nor interpret the motives of their actions any more clearly than you can those of your fellow religious. Therefore do not try to understand these motives; but rather bear in mind what happened to Lot's wife, who, troubled at the perdition of the Sodomites looked back to see what was happening, and punished by God, she turned into a pillar of salt. Keep your soul entirely for God, not suffering the actions of others to disturb your peace of mind. Ascertain the fact that there is no lack of stumbling blocks to be found in religious life, because there is no lack of devils who labor to ruin the work of those striving to become saints. God permits this to happen to try your strength and to show that one cannot be truly religious unless he is entirely detached from all persons. If a religious is not detached, no matter how good his intentions may be, or how great his zeal, sooner or later the devil will ensnare him, overcoming him with violent distractions.
>
> Remember well what St. James says, "If any man thinketh himself to be religious and restrains not his tongue, that man's religion is vain."[1] This refers to both interior and exterior detachment from persons.[2]

The third obstacle which the world sets in contrast to religious perfection is the real or apparent bad example of our brethren in religious life. We have seen that the first obstacle is inordinate affection for any person; the second is disorderly affection for worldly goods; the third is the bad example which we may give to those around us. It was precisely to guard against this danger that St. John wrote the third admonition. It is evident that he considers this third obstacle far more dangerous than the first two because of his lengthy treatment of the subject. Moreover he repeats the same topic in his famous "Four Counsels to a Religious."

Although St. John was a mystic who continually lived in the presence of God, the manner in which he writes indicates his practicality. It likewise reveals his perfect understanding of the defects and dangers which await all human nature. Knowing well the disastrous effects of bad example in religious life he wished his children to be well instructed on the subject and thoroughly prepared to overcome it. If this admonition had not been written by one of St. John's caliber, it might well be misunderstood as being uncharitable to members of religious orders. Since the saints strongly advocate truth they believe that true virtue has nothing to hide. They see and accept persons as they really are and express themselves accordingly. It is in this light that he says: ". . . there is no lack of stumbling blocks in religious houses, because there is no lack of devils who labor to ruin the saints. . . ."

This may be interpreted as meaning that there are some who will always find something of a scandalous nature in religious life. It is necessary to distinguish between the two basic causes of scandal lest we fall prey to our own error. A heart which is not completely purified and filled with charity is very subjective. To him people do not appear as they actually are but rather as a reflection of what he is himself. In this case the cause of the scandal is only in the person scandalized. This explains the words, ". . . If thou considerest any of these things, even though thou livest among angels, many of them will appear to you amiss, since thou wilt not be able to understand the substance of them."[3]

The other cause of scandal is ignorance, or false interpretation of the neighbor's actions. Ninety-nine per cent of the scandals in religious houses originate in ignorance or the subjectivity of the one scandalized. When the soul has not been purified by a thorough knowledge of its own weaknesses, and the heart is not filled with charity one is always looking for defects in his neighbor. This is not true of the saints who are sincere lovers of the truth. Since they are realists they believe that truth has nothing to hide, so they accept things as they are, not as they would like them to be.

At other times the cause of scandal is exterior, as when we actually see someone perform a disedifying action. We are not living with angels but men who are still struggling through the thorns and mire of temptation. Since no one is secure against these dangers as long as he lives in the world, St. John advises both charity and prudence in dealing with our neighbors: "Nor should you ever be shocked or marvel at anything you see or hear, since God permits many devils to strive to overthrow the saints. . . ."[4]

Besides the numerous weaknesses inherent in human nature, there are frequent instigations of the evil spirit against which the Holy Spirit continually admonishes us: "Be sober and watch; because your adversary the devil, as a roaring lion, goeth about seeking whom he may devour."[5] He also informed St. Peter that the devil greatly desired to overpower him: "Simon, Simon, behold Satan hath desired to have you that he may sift you as wheat. But I have prayed for thee, that thy faith fail not; and thou, being once converted, confirm thy brethren."[6] Relative to the temptations to which the Apostles and all men would be subjected Jesus did not ask that the devil might not tempt them, but rather that they would not waiver in the faith. Christ allowed Peter to be tempted and to fall, so that in accordance with the designs of Divine Providence he could better instruct others; ". . . and thou; being once converted, confirm thy brethren." This is the same as if He had said, "By your sad experience with yourself you will better understand the difficulties others experience and you will be better able to help them."

St. John of the Cross explains how fitting it is that God permits the devil to tempt even those souls chosen for the height of love and glory. The justice of God allows this: ". . . so the devil may not allege with truth, that he is given no opportunity for conquering the soul. . . . This would be the case if God did not allow a certain equality between the powers of good and evil, as they both contend for victory in the soul. Then, too, the soul, because of its victory and faithfulness will be more abundantly rewarded."[7]

Such is the high concept of life as seen through the prism of Divine Providence. This is the explanation of the real life of man, of his battles in the moral order, or his painful falls, and of his glorious victories. By being allowed to tempt the good the devil is fulfilling an office entirely proper to him. By allowing him to disclose his refined maliciousness and implacable rage against mankind Divine Providence allows man to fall many times while He is still sustaining them with His divine strength. Thus man still maintains his freedom of choice while the infinite mercy of God dispenses the means of man's increasing patience with himself and showing greater charity toward his neighbor.

St. John of the Cross points out that one of the ways that the evil spirit most frequently tempts men, even those earnestly striving for perfection, is to suggest thoughts relative to their neighbor's faults. The devil represents these faults vividly and falsely, trusting that the weak soul will spread abroad his revelations, thereby adding sin to sin. Then he fills the soul with mistaken zeal by causing it to believe that it has been the recipient of these revelations of weakness so that the soul may commend the person concerned to God. When there is no progress in the erring soul the soul ensnared by Satan easily falls prey to discouragement. The persistent temptations of the devil are very powerful and, at the best, human nature is weak and is subject to many and deplorable falls. While we are living in this world, no matter where we direct our eyes we will see the deficiencies of men, and, if we had the power to look within the recesses of our own souls, we would be overwhelmed by the multitude of serious defects and perhaps even sins that we would find there. These falls produced either by human weakness or the maliciousness and astuteness of the enemy are found even in religious houses since its members are composed of men and not angels. There are, too, souls so lacking in the true spirit of charity that they delight in ferreting out the weaknesses of their neighbor. Thinking themselves free of these defects they reveal the weaknesses of others, not understanding the devious ways of Divine Providence for sanctifying His elect. In this way such souls are guilty of the very faults they criticize in others, while the divine Mercy and Justice has conquered in the very souls believed to be already overcome by Satan.

The root and mother of all vice is pride, and most assuredly this sin, so repulsive and overbearing, does not obtain dominion over anyone without first making him feel that he is less defective and more perfect than his unworthy brethren. There is little profit in concerning oneself with the faults of others if one is well convinced and ashamed of his own faults. Such a soul certainly does not obtain pleasure in accusing another of what he himself is guilty of. Thus David, although bitterly repentant of his own sins could say to God, "It was good for me that you humiliated me, so that I could learn of your justifications."[8] So too, the wise man has said, "What knowledge has he, who has never been tempted? The man tried in many things will be very reflective."[9]

For this reason, then, God allows us to see our brethren fall into sin, not only that we can practice patience and charity but that we may also profit by their example. When we see the defects in others it is only natural that we wonder if we are guilty of the same weaknesses, knowing well that if we do not possess them now, we could very well do so at a later date. St. Paul warns us: "He that thinketh himself to stand, let him take heed lest he fall."[10]

Anyone who is easily scandalized at the faults of his neighbor displays his utter ignorance of the laws of Divine Providence governing the sanctification of souls and demonstrates his lack of knowledge of human weakness. Such a lack of understanding is nothing more than a pretence for criticizing his neighbor, while at the same time it reveals a complete lack of charity. Nothing ever scandalizes the truly great soul, who realizes that the one most harmed by a fault which has been committed is the person himself. The Holy Ghost warns us in this notable passage: "Lie not in wait, nor seek after wickedness in the house of the just, . . . for a just man shall fall seven times and shall rise again."[11] This can be interpreted as saying, "Because you have seen the fall of your brother, who is otherwise good and just, do not make his fault appear greater than it really is. Do not aggravate faults which do not exist except in your own imagination and malice. Do not destroy your neighbor's reputation, for he shall fall and fall many times and just as many times will he rise again, while you, who observe and criticize him only increase your own uncharitableness."

To avoid this evil St. John of the Cross advises and even commands us to remove from our minds any disedifying thought about our neighbor. He wants us to live in the community as if we were entirely alone in the world: "I beseech you to diligently avoid interpreting the actions of the community, much less discussing the events which are none of your concern. This also applies to the individual religious whose character or affairs are none of your concern." St. John uses forceful language warning us that we shall not enjoy peace, even if we lived among angels unless we refrain from what is no concern of ours. He supplements this strong and wise admonition thus: "Even if you were to dwell among devils, God still requires you to live oblivious of their shortcomings, keeping your soul pure and holy in the sight of God, being completely undisturbed by what is transpiring all around you." Since St. John uses such strong language this doctrine must be of the greatest importance.

Before commenting further we would like to explain a misinterpretation which might arise: "If such bad example is thus found in religious and the cloister is not a sufficient safeguard for virtue, then my vocation is not of such great importance." This is illogical reasoning and could be very dangerous to the soul who might believe it. We must remember that a vocation is not the result of a personal whim or caprice. "You have not chosen Me, I have chosen you," said the divine Redeemer to His disciples and He repeats it daily to His religious, "I have chosen you . . . that you should bring forth fruit in due season, and your fruit should remain."[12]

A vocation is a tremendous gift from God to His creature to which He attaches all the graces necessary for personal sanctification. It follows then that the person who does not live up to his vocation will imperil his salvation. Therefore it is foolish for one who has been called to religious life to think he could better achieve his salvation in the world. A religious vocation, however, does not render a person impeccable; rather it is a means of falling less frequently and of rising more easily. When tempted against a religious vocation it is good to call to mind each of the nine advantages that St. Bernard says are attached to it: "In this holy state a man lives more purely, falls more rarely, rises more speedily, walks more cautiously, is refreshed more frequently with heavenly comforts, rests more securely, dies more confidently, is purified more quickly, and rewarded more abundantly."[13]

Consequently, a sincere person will never diminish his appreciation for the religious state regardless of imperfections or bad example. There are and, of necessity must be, temptations in religious life, yet at the hour of death no one regrets having lived in religious life. Let us not, then, cherish anything which would cause us regret at the last hour. Therefore cast aside any temptations which may arise against a religious vocation, thoroughly studying the admonitions of St. John which will insure advancement on the road to perfection.

CHAPTER SEVEN

RASH JUDGMENT

St. John repeats the admonition relative to judgment of one's neighbor in the first of his *Four Maxims to a Religious*. As he says: "Those who fail in charity toward their neighbor fail likewise to profit by any other works of virtue they may perform, and they continually go from bad to worse."[1]

It is sad to think that after many years in religious life one has lost not only the merit of his virtuous actions but has actually fallen into the dangerous state of sin. Let us consider in logical order the evils which may result from a neglect of this important admonition. There is, first of all, a tendency to judge one's neighbor unfavorably, and this is termed "rash judgment." This is equally serious, whether interior or exterior. St. John says that this consists in mental criticism and murmuring resulting in rash statements against one's neighbor. This is corroborated in the celebrated passage of St. James: "If any man think himself to be religious, not bridling his tongue, this man's religion is vain."[2]

In every order, religious, social, or moral, there are certain truths which are fundamental because everyone agrees to them. In secondary truths and the appreciation of details and concrete acts, each one sees them according to his own dispositions. Thus in the actions of our neighbor we see only the external action and know little or nothing of the motives which prompted him to do this act. In order to judge correctly whether a person is worthy of praise or blame, knowledge is a principal requisite. Usually we are ignorant of the true principle of morality guiding the actions of others, therefore it is inevitable that when we judge according to our own light we are often guilty of error.

In every rank of life there are narrow-minded individuals whose horizon is limited to the private and public life of their neighbor. This is not only deplorable but it is a genuine spiritual infirmity.

According to St. Thomas Aquinas, the tendency to judge one's neighbor proceeds from two causes: " . . . either the person is evil-minded and unconsciously judges others by his own evil dispositions or he harbors such envy, hatred, or contempt for his neighbor that he experiences a secret delight in thinking evil of him and readily believes any misconception of his neighbor's actions."[3] This teaching of St. Thomas should teach us to restrain our judgment of our neighbor, because suspicious and unfavorable judgments are a revelation of the infirmities of our own souls. When we are caught by a keen observer in a merciless judgment against our neighbor we should blush at the portrayal of a quality in ourselves which even natural pride would prompt us to conceal. It was St. Bonaventure who said, "When you perceive anything reprehensible in your neighbor, turn your eyes on yourself; before you cast any judgment, examine yourself well, and condemn in yourself that which you would have condemned in him."

If such motives of human respect are insufficient to keep us from rash judgment, then the uneasiness of our conscience should. Concerning the moral aspect of this question St. Thomas states: "Those, who, because of slight indications doubt the goodness of their neighbor, sin venially. If he holds malice against his neighbor and because of this accuses him of wrong, then he is guilty of mortal sin, because of his contempt of his neighbor."[4]

St. Paul is even more severe when he says, "thou art inexcusable O man, whosoever thou art, that judgest. For wherein thou judgest another, thou condemnest thyself."[5] To the Corinthians he adds, "Therefore judge not . . . until the Lord come, who will bring to light the hidden things of darkness."[6] The same exhortation is found in St. Luke: "Condemn not and you shall not be condemned. Forgive and you shall be forgiven. . . . For with the same measure that you shall mete, it shall be measured out to you."[7] Such words are indicative of the fact that on the day of final judgment the same standards will be applied to us personally as we have applied to our fellow men. No matter how incredible it may seem, we know that God, who is all mercy and infinite virtue, judges far more leniently than we oftentimes judge our neighbor. God, knowing and understanding human defects and weaknesses, is ever ready to make all kinds of allowances; thus it is not surprising to read in the Book of Wisdom: "Thou being Master of power, judgest with tranquillity; and with great favor disposeth us . . . but thou hast taught thy people by such works that they must be just and humane. . . ."[8]

Only when man possesses a deep self-knowledge and a broader knowledge of men will he find himself mild in his judgment of others. Yet this is the goal we must strive for, first in our thoughts, since charitable thoughts transform material actions into acts of supernatural value, and this only when we are completely imbued with the spirit of divine love and mercy.

Since God has reserved the right of judgment to Himself, man has no right whatsoever to anticipate the judgment of God and pass sentence on his fellow man, for in so doing he is but condemning himself. Regardless of the actions of our fellow men we must always view them in the spirit of charity and in the realization that "judgment is the Lord's, not man's."

It is true that we nearly always judge without premeditation or malice. Our judgments are usually based on personal antagonism, ignorance, and perhaps a clash of personalities; yet it is not expedient that we rely on such excuses for judging our neighbor. Ignorance may lessen our guilt but at the same time it is equally true that we are bound to regulate our charity and justice toward our neighbor in accordance with God's law of charity. This regulation must begin in the interior since it is our thoughts which govern our speech and our actions. Charitable thoughts will beget charitable words; likewise envious and uncharitable thoughts dispose us to hideous sins against charity and justice.

Everyone is aware from personal experience that rash judgment is moral poisoning. Once the imagination is given free reign then we find evil in others. The insidious poison which we have administered to ourselves increases with each uncharitable thought. We soon find it difficult to be amiable and indulgent toward our fellow religious and as the poison spreads we become more and more intolerant of any weakness, until even the smallest fault becomes magnified to alarming proportions. We can no longer remain master of our speech when we have arrived at this stage because it is always true, "Out of the abundance of the heart the mouth speaketh."[9]

The evils resulting from lack of interior silence and uncharitable speech are without number and God alone knows the damage caused both in the cloister and out of it once this evil has been indulged in. If a rock is dislodged from the top of the mountain, we cannot measure the destruction it will cause until it finally comes to rest in the valley below. This is an apt picture of the slanderous tongue which is a weight from the heart. As it breaks from the sanctuary in which it has been nurtured it hurtles into an abyss which becomes fathomless, leaving bitterness and disaster in its wake. Such words may be filled with resentment and anger, envy and jealousy, but they are always weighted with selfishness, mirroring the narrow soul from which they emerged. They are as arrows shot from one heart to another, communicating to each new victim poison and bitterness. Innocent and pure aspirations become dissipated; souls which have lived in happiness are filled with discontent; but those who have harbored mutual distrust are filled with malice and hatred. What, then, shall stop these icy waves of uncharitableness launched forth by a cold and restless heart in a moment of imprudent confidence? God alone knows, as He alone reads the depths of a human heart.

It is not our intention to study the sins of the tongue in their various forms since volumes are written on this subject. We need only to say that all the evil aspects related to rash judgment are applicable to slander and faultfinding, which evils cover a vaster field than the subject treated here. Rash judgment is self-toxic, whereas slander and faultfinding serve to poison all whom it contacts. Thus a single slanderous word, imprudently uttered, can be more destructive than a drop of poison assimilated by the system, destroying the vital principles of an organic being. Such words cool charity, destroy the most prudent sensibility, and poison the finest sentiments. Each one can study for himself the disastrous effects of backbiting, especially when he hears a person whom he had hitherto esteemed being the subject of such insidious slander. As a result he finds himself becoming suspicious and distrustful, even of his friend, carefully watching for evidences of the evil report. Distrust magnifies the defects of those under observation making it very difficult for us to be outwardly charitable toward them. These sins of the tongue are the worst of all enemies against charity since they ruin peace and confidence. Therefore the Holy Ghost warns us: "A wicked word shall change the heart, making

what is good, evil — what is life, death — and the tongue is the
ruler of them."[10]

Another danger which threatens those occupied in observing the
defects of their neighbors is the consequence of these actions. In
speaking about this St. John cites the example of Lot's wife being
changed into a pillar of salt, claiming that the wretched souls
occupied with other people's actions likewise acquire saline qualities
themselves. Just as salt becomes hard, so too, the soul which
indulges in meddling in another's affairs, becomes hardened and
unkind toward those around him. His haughtiness and intolerance
serve to build a wall of separation between the offender and the
offended, causing numerous unreasonable and illogical judgments
to be passed. Salt is likewise a sign of barrenness; life cannot develop
near rocks of salt. Neither can a soul engaged in uncharitableness
do otherwise than render barren all that they may contact. Their
skill in revealing another's weakness and their hard and merciless
criticisms cause generous hearts to feel completely depressed and
insecure in their company. Near them there is only barrenness,
there is no joy; there is no life.

It is impossible for simplicity and confidence to exist where
restless and uncharitable souls are continually observing others for
the sole pleasure of malicious criticism. Such a spirit is bound to
breed discontent and an attitude of reserve which soon degenerates
into jealousy and suspicion. Eventually the charm of religious life,
which is love and mutual confidence, is destroyed and a rigid formalism replaces the original spirit of peace. Nothing remains but
the letter of the law, that letter, which, according to St. Paul
". . . kills, instead of quickening."[11]

It is certain that while we live among men we shall have to bear
with their weaknesses and they, in turn, will have to bear with ours;
but we must try to live oblivious of the faults which are ever
present in human nature. It is with this in mind that St. John of
the Cross admonishes us to refrain from interfering in the affairs
of our neighbor, to detach ourselves from created objects, and to
regulate our affections toward our fellow men.

Never should the faults of our neighbor be discussed with our
fellow men, unless with one who has the authority to correct the
situation, and then only in the spirit of the greatest charity. This is

insisted on by St. John of the Cross when he says: "Never under the pretext of zeal, or of charity, reveal what we know about our neighbor save to the person who has a right to hear of this, and then with great charity, and at the proper time. . . ."[12]

The habit of practicing the virtue contrary to the fault you have noticed in others produces more effective results than mere words. A prudent and holy superior applied this remedy to an agitated religious who denounced a violation of the rule in another. "I am grateful to you, my dear son, for this zeal for the glory of God and the observance of the rule. Since you are aware of the offense that such a violation has given to God, I willingly grant you permission to fast today in expiation for the fault which has been committed."

If those who are afflicted with undue curiosity about their neighbor's welfare would thus assiduously make reparation for the faults they observe in others, then they would be less inclined to notice the trivial actions of those around them. Doing this would further the plans of Divine Providence to make religious houses the delightful garden where the tree of love would be preserved in its full luxuriance. It is here that Christ meant the great commandment to grow and bear much fruit: "Love one another as I have loved you. . . ."[13]

St. John of the Cross shows us clearly that to be just to God and to fulfill His command of mutual love and understanding we must be merciful to men in thought and deed. Our fraternal charity is then but the fulfillment of our filial piety toward God. Not only in fact, but in reality, Christ has identified Himself with each one of our neighbors so intimately that charity toward our neighbor is but a means of serving Christ Himself. Thus, whether we are living in the cloister or in the world, as long as our hearts remain a garden of delight for Christ through the spirit and practice of charity then ". . . we are the good odor of Christ unto God, . . . to others the odor of life unto life. . . ."[14]

CHAPTER EIGHT

ADMONITIONS AGAINST THE DEVIL

Three admonitions are given against the devil, who is the second enemy of those who are aspiring to perfection. The most ordinary wile used by the devil to deceive even the elect is the appearance of what is evil under the guise of good, because he knows, only too well, that what appears to be evil will always be avoided. One never experiences any misgivings as to what is good if the action is being performed under obedience. Therefore a proper study relative to this matter will bring both security and peace.

The influence of evil spirits over men is certainly not a fancy of ignorant piety or of blind fanaticism. It is a universally accepted belief of mankind, presupposed in many practices of our religion and interwoven into all its fundamental dogmas. If this belief were to be suppressed, we should be compelled to withdraw all our books on piety in order to correct all theology and Catholic liturgy and it would be necessary to re-write the entire Scripture. Our Redeemer Himself says that the enemy who sowed cockle in the field was none other than the devil.[1] And St. Paul exhorts us: "Put you on the armor of God, that you may be able to stand against the deceits of the devil."[2]

The principles of St. John of the Cross in his admonitions against the devil are found clearly and decisively in the following passage of Holy Scripture: ". . . and that great . . . serpent, who is called the devil and Satan, who seduces the whole world, . . . was cast unto the earth and his angels . . . with him. And . . . a loud voice in heaven [was heard] saying: . . . 'Woe to the earth and to the sea because the devil is come down unto you, having great wrath . . . and the dragon was angry against the woman, and went to make war with the rest of her seed, who keep the commandments of God and have the testimony of Jesus Christ.'"[3] The woman against whom the devil vented his anger is the Church and her seed is all men, especially the faithful who keep the commandments and live the testimony of Christ. It would, therefore, be heretical and blasphemous to deny the influence of the devil in the world because it would be contrary both to Scripture and the testimony of Christ Himself.

To admit in theory the possibility of the devil and then in practice to ridicule it as a useful device for frightening ignorant people, is the sign of ignorance and superficial judgment. The great saints and doctors of the Church gave this doctrine the greatest consideration and respect. If it is heretical to deny diabolical influence in the world, it is just as ridiculous to interpret some events of human history as products of the devil. There is room for neither incredulity nor fanaticism in this matter. The truth is very simple to understand. Because of his hatred of God and his diabolical jealousy of man, whom he recognizes as capable of gaining eternal bliss, the devil is filled with an overwhelming desire for our destruction. Each victory gained he counts as an added offense against God because he thus separates the sinner from eternal possession of his greatest Enemy. If he is not successful in achieving complete ruination of a soul, he satisfies himself in doing as much harm as possible, since his one delight is to deprive God of glory and men of their happiness. To succeed in this wicked aim he relies on the tremendous resources of his own nature and the extreme weaknesses of human nature. "The devil provokes us to evil using the world and the flesh as his instruments," says St. Thomas Aquinas.[4]

God does not permit Satan to tempt us beyond our strength, and we know that we can be victorious with the grace of God and our own efforts. Although God in His infinite mercy freely offers eternal life to man, He does not give it to him unless he merits it. "For the rest there is laid up for me a crown of justice,"[5] said St. Paul, and the Lord said to him, "Hold fast that which thou hast, that no man take thy crown."[6] He also said, "He who conquers, to him will be glory and I will share with him my throne."[7] This passage proves then that the crown of justice is not a mere gift but rather a reward. We are cautioned to be vigilant lest someone carry off the crown that has been promised to us. This vigilance presupposes combat which, in turn, requires personal effort. While combat against such a powerful enemy would be futile without divine grace it is logical to conclude that constant co-operation with this grace will merit eternal happiness. This truth is thoroughly understood by the devil, and since he cannot oppose God directly he uses his power and craftiness to destroy, or at least to impair, our co-operation with divine grace.

Satan is more interested in disturbing the good than in presenting new temptations to calloused sinners. These souls he leaves to work out their own perdition through the instrumentality of the world and the flesh, knowing well that one sin is quickly followed by another. His knowledge of the true value of a soul is such that he employs every available artifice to deceive souls using the tactics which best fit the situation. A perfect religious, a saintly sister, a virtuous lay person, are treasures of infinite value. God alone knows fully the true worth of a soul. We humans can only surmise it. A single perfect soul is worth hundreds and thousands of average ones. Such a soul can compensate for all the sins of a community and even of a nation. Of them we can say what was said of our Lord, "He went about doing good."[8] This good is ordinarily diffused silently and without ostentation. Happy the religious house where such a person dwells.

God sometimes permits defects of character and temperament to be visible in such individuals in order to conceal the humility which adorns their souls. Yet despite such obscurity of virtue one cannot long remain unaware of the sanctity which they are bound to radiate.

It is difficult for the devil to ruin those who are seriously resolved to achieve the perfection required of religious. Yet it is not impossible for the devil to attempt to disturb religious causing them much harm and uneasiness. Ordinarily the devil does not succeed in causing a religious to sin mortally, but if he can hinder him from being perfect and keep him in a mediocre state filled with imperfections and venial sins, then he has gained more than if he had induced souls already engulfed in vice to add a hundred or even a thousand links to their chain of perdition. This is the reason why saints and masters of the spiritual life, while making every effort to convert sinners, exert even greater zeal to keep souls on the road to perfection, counseling them minutely against the wiles and deceits of the devil.

From all this it is clear that a person consecrated to God will not consciously remain in the state of sin unless he has already lost his vocation. He may noticeably commit deliberate or isolated faults but he cannot retain an attitude of opposition to his vocation over any period of time. If he does, then he is dominated by the spirit of error to the point where he believes his attitude is perfectly safe and his manner of thinking is preferable to anyone else's. Such an attitude fosters self-esteem, deadens his conscience, encourages pride, foments contempt of neighbor, and daily tends to increase blindness and obstinacy of spirit. St. John remarks, "The devil, too, knows how to penetrate into the soul with a secret self-satisfaction which soon becomes very manifest. He frequently directs his attacks to the senses, setting before the eyes the saints in all their resplendent glory; the ears he fills with magnificent orations and exhortations; to the taste he represents what is most delicious and delectable; all for the sole purpose of producing such intense desires for these things that the soul may be led into great deception and evil."[9]

In another place the saint states: "In his attack on a soul the devil assimilates a guise comparable to that represented by goodness, thus infiltrating himself, like a wolf in sheep's clothing, among the flock with a deception which is barely discernible. Since many things proposed by the devil are in conformity with reason and turn out as described by the devil it is very easy for the soul to be deceived, thinking that this true revelation of the future is the work of God rather than of evil. Such persons are unaware of the natural intelligence of the devil who can easily deduce effect from cause, although both may not always be in agreement since all causes depend upon the will of God."[10] The damage which the malignant spirit thus causes the uncautious is very great. The principal strength of the devil rests in the fact that he mixes truth with lies since he knows that if all were deception he could actually achieve little success. The evil spirit, the archenemy of truth and meekness, knows that the human mind is subject to error especially in matters of morality and that if it persists in this error it will never reach any degree of sanctity simply because such a one lives in ignorance of the true state of his soul. The principle acted on is that if one thing is proved correct, then all is in accord with truth; thus he naturally falls victim to the belief in hundreds of lies.

There are many religious, as well as Christians in the world, who are far removed from the teachings of the Gospel even though they consider themselves better than those who surround them. They not only believe that the only correct way of interpretation is their own but that their actions are the most efficacious means of every good work. The truth is that such egotism and pride supersede any good intentions the person might have, destroying the quality of his actions completely, as the victim becomes increasingly aggressive toward those who hold contrary opinions. This form of supposed good intention is the most powerful weapon the devil can use against the friends of God to disturb and undermine peace and charity within the monastery walls. Such souls would be horrified if they could be made to realize that their so called virtue is nothing more than a refined form of pride, yet it is precisely this pride which permeates and motivates many of their actions. If they could be convinced that the devil himself not only inspires many of their good actions but also takes extreme delight in the state of their soul, they could no longer persist in the error they may have lived in for many years. The glory of God may have occupied the first place in their words but it was the last place in the innermost recesses of their hearts. Thus each supposed act of virtue, which in reality was an act of pride, merited nothing for eternal life. St. John verifies this truth when he says, "There are many Christians in our day who may have certain virtues and perform great actions, yet they merit nothing for eternity since they did not seek the honor and glory which belongs to God alone, but rather the empty satisfaction of their own wills."[11]

A humble prayer for enlightenment and a sincere examination of conscience might bring these persons sufficient grace to convince them that their spirit is not in accord with the Gospel. They may have vowed to follow their divine Redeemer in all things yet their humility, abnegation, and charity certainly do not coincide with His. What more could the evil spirit desire than to frustrate real virtue in the friends of God? For a soul consecrated to God to be satisfied with the avoidance of mortal sin while not striving to progress in religious perfection is symptomatic of religious mediocrity. Such a soul affords the devil a perfect field in which to exercise his deceitful wiles.

If anyone is tempted to disregard this doctrine in whole or in part, then he automatically contradicts St. Paul who tells us that the devil may often disguise himself as an angel of light in order to deceive even the elect. St. John of the Cross, perfectly aware of this truth, thus forcibly states the admonitions necessary to free ourselves from the wiles of the devil.

CHAPTER NINE

RELIGIOUS OBEDIENCE

The first admonition of St. John pertaining to combating the devil is ". . . save when commanded by obligation, perform no act, however good or filled with charity it may appear, whether it be for yourself or for anyone else, without being expressly ordered to do so by obedience. The observance of this law will result in merit and security. Avoid attachment fleeing from the devil and all unknown evils. If you fail to observe this admonition, both in small things as well as greater, no matter how successful you may seem to be, you cannot fail to be completely deceived by the devil. If any action is not the result of obedience then it is worthless, for God prefers obedience to sacrifice. The actions of a religious are not his own, nor to be regulated by his own will, but rather they are to be the result of obedience. Only then will no action be accounted as lost in the eyes of God."[1]

Complete and unhesitating obedience, then, is the first admonition St. John proposes against the craftiness of the devil. He does not tell us never to act against obedience, for this is known to be evil in itself. Rather he wishes all our actions to be so regulated by obedience that we will perform no action without this virtue. Very reasonably St. John requires obedience first because it is a tribute we owe to God, the Creator and Supreme Legislator. To obey God is an act of justice and an acknowledgment of His infinite power and majesty. All great souls, because they are righteous and just, are also obedient. Therefore the Holy Ghost tells us: "The mind of the just studieth obedience."[2] This virtue is most pleasing to God because by it we do not sacrifice our goods but our reason. St. John beautifully states, "One single thought of a man is of greater worth than the whole world, wherefore God alone is worthy of him. . . . The whole world is not worthy of man's thought for it is the work of God alone. Therefore whatever thought of ours is not centered on God is stolen from Him."[3]

By virtue of obedience we have consecrated and subjected to God not only our actions and thoughts but also our reason, the source of our thoughts. Obedience is, therefore, the first and greatest tribute that man can pay to his creator, because it is the tribute of the subjection of reason to God. It is the "spirit of servitude in justice" which the Wise Man wishes to direct the actions of man.

As proof of this, God bestows all His blessings on perfect obedience. If in Abraham He blessed all nations, this was the reward of the submissive and simple obedience of the Holy Patriarch to the voice of God.[4] Perfection without obedience is impossible. Redemption was accomplished through the perfect obedience of Jesus to His eternal Father, who, when He was about to deliver Himself into the hands of His executioners uttered these divine words, "The prince of this world cometh, and in me he hath not anything. But that the world may know, that I love the Father; and as the Father hath given me commandment, so do I. Arise, let us go hence."[5] This great spirit of love and obedience led Him forth to His deliverance into the hands of His enemies. Therefore St. John of the Cross says that perfect obedience is necessary to the attainment of perfection and peace of soul: "That which you seek and that which you most desire you will not find of yourself nor by lofty contemplation, but in deep humility and submissiveness of heart."[6]

It is little wonder then that this great master of the spiritual life should recommend obedience as the necessary and indestructible armor against the evil spirit since it is simple obedience which is the most directly opposed to the diabolical spirit. The motto of Satan and his angels is: "Non serviam."[7] Diametrically opposed to this is the cry with which the divine Redeemer conquered Satan, "Father, not my will, but Thine be done . . . I have come, not to do my will, but Thine."[8]

Since, through the malice of the devil, disobedience and stubbornness have been and still are the source of all evil, Divine Providence has ordained that our redemption and the source of good will depend on obedience and humble submission. "As by the disobedience of one man, many were made sinners; so also by the obedience of one, many shall be made just."[9] To those who rejected the virtue of obedience Christ addressed the following words, "Why do you not know my speech? Because you cannot hear My word.

You are of your father, the devil, and the desires of your father, you will do. . . . When he speaketh a lie, he speaketh of his own; for he is a liar, and the father thereof."[10] According to this infallible testimony of uncreated Truth, the devil is the father of lies, as well as the father of all disobedience. Therefore all souls rebellious to the voice of God are children of the devil.

Once when Christ was preaching, it was announced to Him that His Mother was waiting to see Him. He answered, " 'Who is my mother, and who are my brethren?' And stretching forth His hand toward His disciples, He said: 'Behold my mother and my brethren. For whosoever shall do the will of my Father that is in heaven, he is my brother and sister and mother.' "[11] This passage contains the greatest and fullest praise of obedience that has ever come to the human ear, just as the foregoing passage contained the most terrible anathema against disobedience and stubbornness. Let us remember that He, who spoke this way is Christ, our Lord, who cannot exaggerate in praising or in censuring, because He is infinitely true and just. If the children of Satan are cast aside, it is because they are disobedient and stubborn; while the sincerely obedient are reckoned among the chosen family of God. Each of these souls is to Christ His brother, His sister, and His Mother. The Blessed Virgin was so dear to Christ, not only because she was His mother but even more because she was the creature of God who most perfectly accomplished His will. Thus the eulogy which our Lord bestowed on the virtue of obedience should more than suffice to make every religious love obedience.

All great saints taught, respected, and practiced obedience because they recognized it as the real foundation of the religious life and the social order. Without such obedience to law and authority it is not possible to find civic virtue in society, Christian virtue in the Church, and still less monastic virtue in religious houses. Charity and obedience are of greater importance in the religious than in the moral order. Charity is essential because all virtues are related to it as the crown of religious practices. Obedience is important because without it as a foundation, there is nothing solid on which to build. Man is never so great as when he bows his head to obey: "The sons of wisdom," says the Holy Ghost, "are the church of the just: and their generation, obedience and love."[12] God always blesses the obedient and renders their works fruitful. That is why Sacred Scripture tells us: "An obedient man shall speak of victory."[13] Speaking on the same subject a venerable English bishop said, "It is a special gift to know how to succeed in every enterprise, and this seems to be the reward of obedience, for God blesses every action which is undertaken by holy obedience."[14]

The efficacy and merit of our actions lies in the spirit in which they are executed while the moral value rests on the interior submission to Him in whose honor they are performed. A little work done in the spirit of obedience is of infinite value to him who performs it and may even be the beginning of great deeds. Frustrated talent is found all over the world. Religious orders and the Church itself, on the contrary, are filled with great works accomplished by the simple and the humble who perform them in the virtue of holy obedience. It follows, then, that no matter how excellent the work might be in itself, a religious who does not perform it under obedience is definitely wasting his time.

In the old Testament we find examples of the Israelites offering many excellent sacrifices and holocausts to God. Equally great was their spirit of fasting. Yet God was not pleased with these actions. We read in Isaias of the Israelites' complaint, "Why have we fasted and thou hast not regarded us? Why have we humbled our souls and thou hast not taken notice? . . ." And the Lord answered them, "Behold in the day of your fast your own will is found."[15] It was as if He had indeed said to them, "I know that you have fasted and have offered Me many victims, but all this is good and commanded in the law. You have not done these things in submission to My will, but only because they were pleasing to you."

It is, therefore, no wonder that St. John of the Cross, speaking of those who perform great penances without permission, wrote the following severe passage: "These persons are most imperfect and devoid of reason, for they set bodily penance before subjection and obedience which is the penance of the reason and therefore constitutes a sacrifice which is far more acceptable and pleasing to God. To disregard obedience is to perform the penance of the irrational because the only attraction concerned is the pleasure and personal satisfaction which is found in the action."[16]

It is to be noted that this severe reprimand was written by the austere reformer of Carmel, the great lover of the cross who was the greatest miracle of penance in modern times. What would he say of those who show their disregard for this virtue by performing positive acts against it? What would he think of those who undertook great penances yet performed actions more or less forbidden either by the rule or the superior?

St. Theresa agrees thoroughly with St. John in the matter of obedience. "If anyone is under the vow of obedience and still goes astray because she failed to observe the slightest implication of this vow, I do not know why she is in religious life. I can assure her of this, however — that as long as she fails in obedience she will never succeed in living a contemplative life, or even of living a good active life. Of this I am absolutely certain."[17]

All the saints regarded obedience as the basis of all Christian virtue, the necessary foundation of community life, and the sanctification of the individual. If this foundation is undermined, even in the minutest detail, the whole edifice will collapse. A religious without true obedience will never become perfect, and a religious congregation in which the bonds of obedience are relaxed will shortly find itself sentenced to death, unless the matter is immediately remedied. Little wonder, then, that St. John warns us: "Save when commanded by obedience perform no act, no matter how good and virtuous it may appear to be, whether it be for thyself or for anyone else within or without the community."[18]

St. Theresa adds to this exhortation, "I believe it is the devil, who, seeing that there is no path which leads more quickly to the height of perfection than obedience, suggests all these objections and difficulties under the guise of good. Let this be carefully noted and the truth of the matter will be most evident."[19]

St. Bonaventure does not hesitate to declare that all religious perfection consists in the perfect abnegation of one's will, i.e., in perfect obedience. For this reason also, the greatest of the vows and the only one whereby man may deliver himself completely into the hands of God, is the vow of obedience. By the vow of poverty we give God our goods; by the vow of chastity we renounce sensual pleasures, but by the vow of obedience we renounce the greatest of man's faculties, his will. The renunciation of our reason and liberty constitute the total sacrifice of man to God. Furthermore, what has once been given to God cannot lawfully be reclaimed. This is evident from the teachings of St. John when he says: "The actions of a religious are not his, for they belong to obedience. If he withdraws from this, they will be accounted as lost. Carefully consider that if God exacts from the faithful a strict account of any idle word, how much more will He not exact an account far more rigorous from a religious whose whole life has been consecrated to Him?"[20]

These words of Sacred Scripture are applicable to religious: "To rebel is like the sin of witchcraft; to refuse to obey is like the crime of idolatry."[21] Once a person has consecrated his will, his liberty, and his entire person to God any action performed without obedience is dedicated, not to God but rather to his own caprices, and this brings great dishonor to God. If God were so angry with the sons of Heli because their sacrifice was incomplete, how much more displeased will He justly be with the religious who, having entirely consecrated his will to God, reclaims it, wishing to act according to the desires of his own heart rather than according to the dictates of obedience?

It is not sufficient merely to keep the vow of obedience; it is also necessary to acquire the virtue of obedience. The vow is the means, the virtue is the end. Means which do not lead to the end are useless; likewise the vow of obedience has no value before God if it does not incline the religious to a perfect interior submission to His will manifested by the rule or his legitimate superiors. Social and civic bodies lay down laws more or less just, and every self-respecting person observes them exactly. It is a question of honor to be obedient to such laws. Yet this is not religious obedience, which is to be found more in the spirit than in external actions.

"Obedience may be interpreted as a course of action, or it may mean the interior impulse with which one acts. Both adaptations must be realized by the religious, for the life of obedience is based on the spirit which motivates it. A religious may obey through mere habit, by routine, for the sake of a peaceful life, or through mere slavishness of disposition. Such a person outwardly leads an obedient life, but he is not obedient, because inwardly he is in the state of rebellion." This passage of the venerable prelate, Bishop Hedley, well deserves a little application. No religious is obedient unless his exterior performance is the reflection of an interior submission to the will of God intimated to him by the rule or by his superior. It does not matter that his exterior actions are in perfect harmony with the command, or that he moves within the sphere assigned with the same precision as the hands of a clock. Such exactitude might be sufficient for civic virtue but it is not for a religious. External submission of the will may make a good servant, an excellent employee, or a perfect soldier, but it is not enough to make even a mediocre religious.

By the vow of obedience we have made an offering of our person and liberty to God; but God, unlike men, is not satisfied with appearance, as He tells us by His prophet: "But thou, O Lord of Sabbaoth, . . . judgest justly, and triest the reins and the heart."[22]

Essential for religious perfection is an interior spirit of total submission. It is with this in mind that St. John advises us: ". . . Though you perform many actions there will be no progress in perfection unless you learn to deny your own will, submitting yourself perfectly to the will of your superiors."[23]

Only when our will is in complete accord with the will of God will our union with God be complete. It is in seeing God's will in all commands given to us by superiors that we find the secret root of the apostolic fruitfulness of Carmel, as well as any religious life: "On Mount Carmel, God alone and I. God alone in my spirit to enlighten it; God alone in my acts to sanctify them; God alone in my heart to possess it."[24]

CHAPTER TEN

THE VOW AND VIRTUE
OF OBEDIENCE

As we have seen from the preceding chapter, a religious cannot be considered really obedient who is wanting in the interior spirit of submission, even though he exteriorly does all that is commanded of him. Neither can he expect any reward for his actions if he tries to escape any commands contrary to his desires by employing a thousand little artifices, more or less reprehensible in themselves. Even though such a religious does not violate the vow of obedience his unrestrained liberty cannot allow him to be considered obedient in the eyes of God.

In order to obtain the reward promised for obedience it is not sufficient merely to observe all that is carefully commanded or forbidden by obedience under pain of mortal sin. It is also necessary to keep in mind the thousand minor regulations which constitute the framework of religious life. There is an infinite distinction between the spirit of perfect obedience and the observance necessary for the fulfillment of the formal precepts of the vow of obedience. On the one hand, we have the example of our divine Lord to whom the wind and the sea were subservient, to whom the angels, good and evil, were bound to give submission because He was the Son of God. Yet He, who was the complete Master of all, ". . . humbled Himself becoming obedient unto death, even to the death of the cross."[1] On the other hand, we have the ecclesiastical and moral laws which point out to the religious the strict precepts of the vow of obedience saying to them: "If you go beyond this you violate grievously the most fundamental of the religious vows; you burden your conscience with a mortal sin, and you become liable to all the rigors of the law."

Fortunately, however, in religious houses, it is very seldom that one transgresses grievously either the vow of obedience or any of the other vows. As there are comparatively few souls who reach the high degree of perfect obedience wherein their will coincides identically with the will of God, so there are fewer still who deliberately break the vow of obedience in matters formally commanded by the rule or the superior. The majority of religious may be classified between these two extremes; they neither practice consummate virtue nor fall into complete degradation. A mediocre religious does not wish to overstep the limits beyond which an act would be considered sinful. Others are so far removed from obedience that they scarcely know how to take the first step toward the attainment of this virtue, but merely fulfill the letter of the law and nothing more. If one were to continually walk near a thorny hedge he would be in continued danger of being pricked by the thorns. In the same manner a mediocre religious is more concerned with finding a means of doing his own will while still not conspicuously violating his vow of obedience.

Another group of religious follow an obedience which is strictly servile. They are continually striving to avoid the ill-will of their superiors while simultaneously they are enjoying the liberty of following their own whims and fancies. Instead of trying to purify themselves from their imperfections or studying how they can better serve God, they are always on the alert to circumvent any trying obedience which may be assigned to them. In this way they do not clash with their own consciences nor with their self-love, because they honestly believe that since they are outwardly fulfilling the claims of obedience they are not wrong, while all the time they are doing nothing but their own will. The condition of such a soul is lamentable. It is true that in their state of conscience there is no single action which may be qualified as a mortal sin, but in some respects their condition is worse for they lack the stimulus to arouse remorse of conscience.

The inhalation of foul air over a period of time poisons an entire organism so that little by little it dies. This is the picture of a tepid religious whose languid way of living is nothing more than slow spiritual death. How can such lives, even though apparently free from mortal sin, be offered to divine Justice to compensate for the sins of the world? Yet this is precisely what the special graces attached to religious life are meant to do, and it is one of the purposes for which religious congregations were founded. A religious who, apart from clearly defined mortal sin, holds back as much as he can of what he had once freely donated to God, will surely not make any atonement for the sins of others, rather he will provoke the divine wrath upon himself. God cannot be pleased with those who seem incapable of doing either good or evil; who feel neither horror for mortal sin nor the salutary effects of ardent charity. God tells us in the Apocalypse how He considers such persons: "I know thy works, that thou art neither cold nor hot . . . but because thou art lukewarm, and neither cold nor hot, I will begin to vomit thee out of my mouth."[2] Certainly no religious would like to have such words applied to him. Yet it is clear that they are addressed to the mediocre who though not laden with mortal sin still did not experience the fervor of charity. Our Lord completely rejects those who are guilty of grievous sin. The lukewarm eventually become so deformed in His sight that the divine Mercy, so tolerant of the weaknesses of men, can no longer hold them within the embrace of His love and He is forced to cast them away. Such words found in Sacred Scripture should fill us with a salutary fear. Yet who are more lukewarm than those who never give their will entirely to God, although they have consecrated it to Him by the vow of obedience? God is not so much interested in the goods we give Him by the vow of poverty, nor in our body consecrated to Him by the vow of chastity, nor in all the other religious mortifications we may offer Him. All these are only means leading to the true and real sacrifice of our own will. If we deprive Him of this sacrifice, what else remains of value in the religious life?

When these poor religious who have been so zealous for their own will present themselves before their Judge to give an account of the fruit of their labor, they might well use these apparently simple but terrifying words condemning themselves: "Lord, during my entire religious life I have tried often to do my own will, and many times I have succeeded. Yet in so doing I have never openly violated my religious vows." Surely such an account will not serve as a consolation to the tepid religious. The first and most necessary obligation of every religious is to keep his vows intact and this is possible only by the faithful observance of obedience which is the foundation of all other virtues. A religious may never have violated his vows of obedience nor poverty; he may never have openly rebelled against his superior or against his rules; he may never have used nor kept anything as his own; but if he has never performed any positive acts of virtue he cannot be said to be an obedient or docile religious. What reward can he expect for his religious life? He will be treated as the man who was sent in the morning to work in the garden and at eventide had nothing to show for it, even though he may have worked diligently.

Christ said to His Apostles, "I have chosen you, and have appointed you that you should go, and should bring forth fruit."[3] To the disciple who returned from his mission very much satisfied because he had not lost his talent, although he had not traded it either, our Lord said, "Take . . . the talent from him and give it to him who hath ten talents. For to everyone who hath, shall be given, and he shall abound. But . . . the unprofitable servant cast ye out into the exterior darkness."[4] Comparable to this unprofitable servant is the religious who has never broken his vow of obedience. but neither has he endeavored to acquire the virtue of obedience. He has buried his talent of obedience in the earth and has produced nothing.

The root buried deep in the soil and nurtured with seasonable rains will bring forth the shoot, from the shoot come the branches, from the branches the flowers and the fruit. The vow of obedience is the bitter root which must be deeply buried for it is the interior immolation of our will to God. Properly guarded and cultivated it must, as a natural result, produce the most delicate flowers and exquisite fruits. Perfect obedience contains all the other virtues, and the obedient religious, blessed by God, never ceases to please God and to bring blessings upon his order. Such is the ideal religious.

There are great and wonderful advantages to the obedient in spirit. The religious knows that in obeying he is doing what pleases God the most. St. Theresa considered it a great blessing to bind herself by vow to do always what she understood to be most perfect. Those who have the good fortune of being under obedience in all the details of their life, know that to do what is commanded them is the most perfect for themselves while at the same time they are bringing great honor and glory to God.

An obedient religious receives merit for all his actions, whether they are menial or very lofty, since merit does not depend on what a person does, but why he does it. If the only motive of his actions is the will of God manifested to him by His legitimate representatives, he merits as much as he who does the highest and most honorable action in the eyes of the world. Furthermore he is free from the innumerable anxieties about the success of his work or the bitter disappointment of failure. Whoever works under obedience never fails because obedience never fails. Deeds activited by obedience are acceptable to God and if a religious does all in his power to achieve the desired end then he is successful. All other results are of secondary value. He who obeys has the right to divine assistance; for the obedient does not act in his own name but in the name of God. Therefore when he has done all that he can do, he can say to the Lord: "Lord, I have done my part, what remains is Thine." Finally, obedience renders us in a certain sense impeccable, for as St. John says: "He who does not seek his own will, nor his own pleasure, nor the pleasures that come from God or creatures, but seeks only the will of God will never stumble."[5]

In order to weaken the power of Satan relative to obedience it is necessary to understand perfectly the admonitions of St. John, ". . . and if you do not observe this admonition in both small and great things, no matter how successful the results may be, you cannot fail to be deceived by the devil. If you do nothing other than fail to be ruled in all things by obedience, you stray and are worthy of blame."[6]

When we find obedience difficult and almost unreasonable, then we should bring to mind this admonition of St. John. At such times it is evident that the devil is seeking to overpower us or at least to deprive us of the merit of obedience. He knows that we will not succumb to evil as such so he offers the poison under the appearance of good.

It is fitting to close this chapter with some passages from St. Theresa: "Do not forget that the devil employs every artifice to overcome those dwelling in religious houses. He will particularly strive to tempt you regarding obedience. Therefore be on your guard in such thoughts as these: But I am a senior religious; but I am older; but I have worked harder; but the other sister is being treated better than I. When such thoughts arise check them quickly otherwise they will give rise to other and more serious abuses. The remedy for this evil is to be found in earnest and trusting prayer because the very day you cease to pray spiritual degradation will set in. . . . Let us strive to imitate the humility of the most sacred Virgin whose habit we wear. At the same time let us remember that no matter how much we may advance in humility we still fall far short of the humility possessed by the Mother of God."[7]

CHAPTER ELEVEN

SUPERIORS AND OBEDIENCE

The second admonition advises us to look upon the superior, whoever he may be, as one taking the place of God. The summary of St. John's text relative to this matter follows: "Consider the superior as the representative of God and you will profit greatly; if you do not do so, then you will suffer a great loss. Do not then attempt to interpret his actions, habits, or characteristics, pleasing or otherwise, for if you do, then you will be exchanging the obedience of God for human obedience. You will be more influenced by the visible characteristics of the superior than by the invisible God whom you should serve in his person. Such obedience is vain and unfruitful, meriting nothing in the eyes of God. The devil, the enemy of humility has ruined the perfection of a great number of religious by causing them to consider only human characteristics. You must strive to lay aside personal feelings, regarding each superior as the representative of God and nothing more. If you do not, then you will never achieve spirituality nor remain faithful to the practice of your vows."[1]

These words of St. John are so tremendous that they merit the greatest attention of every religious. He commands us, ". . . never consider the superior as less than God, regardless of who he may be . . .", and he assures us that the devil has caused the ruination of those who fail to keep this precept. To do so a religious will not only lack spirituality himself but he will not be able to keep his vows consistently. It can readily be seen that one is not free to accept or reject this admonition since both individual and community sanctification depend upon it.

It is unfortunate that subordinates with little virtue are often scandalized by the shortcomings of their superiors, yet it is clear that no superior would want to be a scandal to these weak souls whom the Lord has entrusted to him. Therefore it seems expedient to remind superiors to watch assiduously, so that in the discharge of their duties their shortcomings will not be apparent to their subjects. Since half-truths are dangerous and useless, it is better to accept the entire truth relative to this matter in the spirit of charity. ". . . subjects may never fix their attention on the personal defects of their superiors; neither may superiors try the virtue of their subjects by their personal defects." Since both issues must be faced honestly a few simple reflections will be made on superiors before commenting on the perfect obedience owed to them by their subjects. What is said is not stated in the spirit of criticism of, or in opposition to, authority, because in the course of twenty years the author has held the office of superior in one form or another.

The admonition states that religious have a serious obligation of overlooking the personal qualities of their superiors, and of fixing their minds on God alone, whom the superior represents. No matter what we may do to stimulate ourselves to put this into practice or to inculcate it into others we shall always fall far short of the reality.

Honor as well as authority is conferred upon those who receive the office of superior since every legitimate superior is invested with lawful power. St. Paul states that all authority is from God; therefore every superior is the representative of God, especially while he is dispensing the duties of his office. The words of the Gospel are most applicable to all legitimate superiors: "He that heareth you, heareth me; and he that despiseth you, despiseth Me; and he that despiseth Me, despiseth Him that sent Me."[2] Those given charge of souls are delegated by Divine Providence for the greatest and most important work in the world, which is the greater glory of God made possible by the sanctification and salvation of souls. The position of a superior relative to his subject is that of a divinely appointed coadjutor, and for this reason they always occupy a pre-eminent place according to the words of St. Paul: "Let [those] who rule well be esteemed worthy of double honor."[3]

It would be a fault if a superior were to consider only his right to honor or pre-eminence and to overlook his power of example. Authority elevates the individual but the higher the office the more one becomes exposed to the public eye. While one mingles with the multitude it is easy to conceal one's imperfections, but when a person is elevated ever so little, even his smallest defect becomes glaring. We often see individuals who, loved and esteemed by all while they were in a humble position, suddenly become despised and dishonored when elevated to a high position. The reason for this is that man is unwilling to honor those whose defects dishonor the position they hold. There is no better gauge than authority to learn the true value of a person. The wise man gives us this prudent counsel: "Have they made thee ruler? Be not lifted up! Be among them as one of them."[4]

There is no one at hand to oblige a superior to observe the law. His chief rule of conduct is his conscience. He enjoys, therefore, more liberty, and liberty is the true test of a person's character. Good educators say that the best means of learning the disposition of children is to allow them complete liberty; so to learn the real value of a person there is nothing like the office of superior. To hold this office for several years and not lead a wasted life is a sign of great virtue and deep spirituality. Any person who uses his office simply to satisfy his own desires is an object of the deepest pity, and he will most surely lose his reputation in the eyes of his subjects.

Good superiors, far from believing that they are permitted certain liberties on account of their office, consider themselves more restricted than their subjects, who by simply asking the superior's permission render their actions lawful and meritorious. Mere lawfulness does not suffice for a superior; he needs tacit and full consent from his subjects and this is not easily obtained. Superiors must bear in mind the words of that great model of superiors, St. Paul: "All things are lawful to me, but all things are not expedient."[5]

Our Lord Himself personally appointed the first superior of His Church but before doing so He questioned Peter three times as to his love: "Lovest thou Me? Lovest thou Me, more than these?" This question put by God to one of His creatures is simply overwhelming, bringing man to his knees in adoration of the God who has such a tender love for His creatures. Such a question touches man so intimately that when he becomes cognizant of its real meaning he finds it impossible to give a coherent answer. Twice, without realizing the full import of the question asked, St. Peter boldly declared his love for Christ. It took the penetrating glance of Christ to completely transform the soul of St. Peter so that his final reply defied the mere expression of words. He, who was the first Apostle, the first superior of the Church and the model of all others, could speak only in the language of love as with all the fervor of his heart he cried: "Lord, Thou knowest all things; Thou knowest that I love Thee."[6] Not until the sublime question was answered in this manner was the ineffable precept "feed my sheep" intimated to Peter.

This scene signifies the need of the superior's being a man of great understanding, capable of lavishing affection on each individual. The greater love he has for his subjects the greater a superior he becomes. The rule itself is rigorous enough and if it is not softened by the goodness and love of the superior, then he surely endangers his own authority and places obstacles in the way of his subjects because religious are especially in need of kind and affectionate treatment. Let us emphasize this point: every human being suffers from a longing for affection, even when we are convinced that we do not deserve it. No matter how spiritual a man may become, he is bound to react to manifestations of affections from one whom he respects and esteems.

During the first year of the author's religious life he minutely studied the reactions of a fellow religious who had been the recipient of outstanding literary honors. So greatly did he desire the esteem of all that he could scarcely bear a reprimand. A poor condemned criminal, whom the writer assisted, told him: "I do not mind dying; what I mind most is to die without having anyone's affection. There will not be a single person to shed a tear over my body or to erect a cross over my grave." When he was assured that this was not so, he not only ascended the steps of the gallows with resignation but with joy.

This illustrates the need of every human being for affection. No matter how perverse a man may seem to be, he would improve if he could be convinced that he is still able to give and to receive the pure affection known to him in his childhood.

One of the greatest treasures peculiar to religious life is the bond of affection between the superior and subject which is manifested in the title "father" (or "mother") with all that this connotes. Since the love of a superior is not disturbed by natural relationships it is peaceful, yet no less sweet nor intense. In youth, when the heart and the imagination are still in their pristine freshness, and all is bright and smiling with happiness it is very easy to cultivate friendship within the limits of a pure and sincere affection, and to believe that this love is natural. But in later years, when much labor has affected the spirit and the heart in such a way that all this seems far from us, then it is a blessing to be able to trust with filial confidence a man who has not the right to cast us aside, and who, we know, takes pleasure in receiving us as a father does a son.

Precisely because we esteem the superior as a father we kneel to receive his blessing before retiring at night. Surely no religious would like to die without the fatherly blessing of his superior. Yet if sincerity is missing and we are not sure of the paternal love of the superior, all this becomes a farce and the observance of religious discipline is increasingly more difficult. Even the bravest of generals feels happy when he can receive the blessings and caresses of his mother. So too, religious, both young and old, feel happy when they are loved by their superior. To act in this manner at all times places a great demand upon the superior. What is most valuable is always the most difficult to obtain and the greatest moral power of man lies in his heart. Therefore a sincere paternal love, so strong that it endures and obliges one to forget and sacrifice himself completely is perhaps the greatest moral miracle. In the natural order the love necessary for the existence of the human family is instilled into the hearts of the parents, especially into the heart of a mother. In the supernatural order such a love is also necessary for the well-being of the religious, so God bestows this gift of paternal love on all superiors.

Paternal love constitutes one of the greatest difficulties in the proper discharging of a superior's duties. If a superior could always control his heart, if he could conserve the youthful love of the saints and the affection which softens every hardship, then indeed his office would not be difficult. Youthfulness of heart is as difficult to preserve as youthfulness of body, and without a very special grace it is impossible. Every man must lament, more or less, with David: "My iniquities have overtaken me, and I was not able to see. They are multiplied above the hairs of my head: and my heart hath forsaken me."[7]

There are relatively few superiors who fail to attend to the requests of their subjects. But this is not enough; the title of charity obliges him to a greater charity than this. It necessitates a searching out of the ones who do not come to him, or even avoid him. By virtue of his office he must seek out such souls doing all in his power to convince them of his fatherly solicitude. This is very difficult at times since there is a natural antipathy toward some individuals. Some persons because of mannerisms, education, character, or particular idiosyncrasies may naturally irritate the superior. God permits such things to happen for the greater exercise of charity. Some souls because of their dissatisfaction frequently and unintentionally mortify others very much. Everything disturbs them and they aggravate everyone else. The attitude of such religious before a superior may be an exterior practice of the teachings of the Gospel but interiorly it is filled with self-love and doomed to destruction. Such persons are most assiduous in observing the exterior details of discipline and most vigilant that nobody else violates them, thus setting themselves up as judges of all things and of all persons. Undoubtedly the first victim of their zeal is the superior. His real defects are highly magnified and his best intentions misinterpreted. They will not go so far as hatred, of course, since there is no room in a religious house for hate, yet on the other hand they will do all in their power to make the superior most uncomfortable. These are the superior's hours of probation; in them he is purified. The counsel will be offered to abandon such ingrates until they are converted, or perhaps to turn their tactics on them in retaliation. But what does conscience say? "You must be a father to them, and even more. You must not forsake your children in this hour of darkness nor seek revenge." Carnal prudence will whisper many things and make diverse suggestions to wounded self-love but the charity of Christ will tell us that such souls may well be passing through a crisis and be totally unaware of the harm they are inflicting. Christian prudence will counsel us not to forsake them but to avail ourselves of every opportunity to enlighten their minds and to remove the bitterness from their hearts. Deep understanding, love, and confidence will do much to convert such trying souls.

This clearly proves the many sacrifices demanded of the office of superior. To sacrifice one's susceptibilities for those who return no love, to love always with affectionate goodness those to whom we are naturally adverse surpasses the ordinary strength of the human

heart. It is then that the prayer of the superior should be the echo
of David: "Have mercy on me, O God . . . create a clean heart in
me and renew a right spirit within me. Cast me not away from Thy
face, and take not Thy holy spirit from me. Restore unto me the
joy of Thy salvation and strengthen me with a perfect spirit."[8]

Such hours of desolation are bound to afflict the lives of every
superior and no relief will be found save in humble and fervent
prayer. Then will they come to a more perfect understanding of the
sobs and groans of the first superior of God's people, Moses, who,
notwithstanding the great solicitude for his people, saw them
dissatisfied and murmuring against God and himself. He turned
toward God with the words which betrayed the profound bitterness
of his soul. "Why hast thou afflicted thy servant? Wherefore do I
not find favor before Thee? Why hast Thou laid the weight of all
this people upon me? Have I conceived all this multitude, or
begotten them, that Thou shouldst say to me: 'Carry them in thy
bosom as the nurse is wont to carry the little infant, and bear
them into the land for which thou hast sworn to their fathers.' "[9]

Ingratitude cannot be offered as an excuse; for reward is to be
expected from God alone. Lack of amiability on the part of a
subject does not excuse a lack of charity, for one must be loved
for the love of God, not for the qualities he possesses.

Superiors should frequently meditate on this passage from the
prophet Ezekiel: "And the word of the Lord came to me, saying:
'Son of man, . . . Prophesy, and say to the shepherds . . . of Israel
that fed themselves: . . . My flock you did not feed. The weak
you have not strengthened, . . . that which was broken you have
not bound up, and that which was driven away you have not
brought again, . . . but you ruled over them with rigor and harsh-
ness. Therefore, ye shepherds, hear the word of the Lord, I, myself,
. . . require my flock at their hands.' "[10]

Greater than the responsibilities entailed in administration is
the powerful influence a superior wields over others. Ecclesiasticus
tells us that as the ruler of the city is, such also are they who dwell
therein. It could well be that the good example of a superior will
not be imitated by many, but his bad example will merit legions
of followers. In Holy Scripture we read the intimation that ruin
will come upon nations because of impotent rulers, "I will give
children to be their princes. . . ."[11] How much more so will inept

superiors bring ruination to religious communities. To all subjects St. Paul may say, "Obey your prelates, and be subject to them. For they watch as having to render account of your souls."[12] But to superiors, who have a tremendous responsibility before God, the Holy Ghost warns: "A most severe judgment shall be for them that bear rule."[13]

St. Theresa regarded the office of superior with extreme trepidation. This is proved from the incident of a holy superior who had lived and died in a holy manner. Yet when she heard of his death she was greatly troubled for the salvation of his soul for that religious had been a superior for twenty years. "This," she exclaimed, ". . . always causes me misgivings for it seems to me a dangerous thing to have charge of souls."[14] At the same time let us notice the charity of this saint who ". . . greatly distressed went to an oratory and there offered on his behalf all the good I had done in my whole life, which was comparatively little, and then I begged our Lord to make up for the deficiencies of this soul with His own merits."[15] She goes on to relate that after fifteen days she saw his soul rise from purgatory to heaven in great glory. This religious of exemplary life was not released from purgatory until the Lord Himself had made up for what was wanting for the ransom of his soul! If this is true of a soul eulogized by St. Theresa, what shall we say of the amount of time we of ordinary virtue will have to spend in purgatory?

The office of a superior is, then, fraught with many dangers. It imposes great and continuous sacrifices and entails tremendous sacrifices. Hence, it cannot be accepted except under strict obedience, for only then will it bear with it the merits and blessings of God.

CHAPTER TWELVE

THE SUBJECT AND OBEDIENCE

From the foregoing admonitions we are aware that the best and most effective means against the strategies of our enemy and our own weakness, is a blind and prompt obedience to the will of God. This is manifested by the rule or the will of our superior. The superior is the messenger of God to man in as much as he is obliged by virtue of his office to point out God's will for each individual's sanctification. In the same way religious must not consider the person of the superior, but only what he orders, because as long as he does not command anything contrary to the spirit of the rule, his order is from God in whose Name he commands. Herein lies the secret of sanctification. This is evident in a celebrated letter of St. John of the Cross in which he writes: "What a religious does by obedience in little things is more pleasing to God than if he performed great virtue and difficult things without the sanction of obedience."[1]

The acquisition of this beautiful ideal requires a lifetime of effort. Yet as religious we have chosen perfect obedience as our final goal, consequently our conscience and our honor requires that we continually strive to achieve perfect submission of will to the will of God. To fail to do this is to fill our lives with many obstacles and sorrows.

For religious it is not necessary to consider actions that are openly rebellious against the formal precepts of obedience, because such acts are rarely to be found among persons consecrated to God. Only in cases of the greatest importance can a formal precept of obedience be imposed by any superior and consequently open rebellion is almost unknown in a religious house. There is, however, another rebellion far more dangerous, because it is more subtle and more difficult to recognize. It is not a disobedience that is visible, but rather an interior antipathy directed against the spirit of obedience. Such disobedience is not manifested by external violent opposition to either authority or the rule, but there is a secret rebellion against submission to authority which is not manifested exteriorly. This type of disobedience covers such a vast area that it can extend to all points of the rule and to every command of the superior, thus rendering the lack of observance far more dangerous than an open act of rebellion. This subtle antagonism has the power of transforming actions, trivial in themselves, into occasions of grievous sins since they gnaw at the very core of religious obedience. The Angelic Doctor leaves no doubt in one's mind when he says, "Whoever, breaking a point of the law, despises authority or makes the attainment of the law impossible is guilty of mortal sin."[2]

Therefore, apart from open rebellion against the rule or the command of superiors formally intimated, which happens rarely, there are two ways in which religious can commit mortal sins against the obedience they have vowed to God. The seriousness of the first lies in the fact that the transgression includes a contempt of law or of authority; in the second, the transgression frustrates the end intended by the legislator.

The end which Christ intended to result from the gift of a religious vocation, was, and is, perfect charity. This unquestionably means we must love God above all things and our neighbor as ourselves. Since contempt is essentially opposed to both of these commandments it follows that any action which is based on contempt is the basis of mortal sin. St. Thomas explains this with his customary clearness. "There is contempt for authority when one disobeys, not through fickleness, nor inattention, nor because the mind is disturbed by passion, anger, or some inordinate affection. The fault lies in the lack of complete submission of the will. This does not mean that frequent transgressions against obedience indicate a state of mortal sin, nor a defiance of authority but this frequency does dispose a person toward contempt and ultimate mortal sin." From these clear premises it is easy enough for the individual to draw the proper conclusion.

There are some consciences which are in such a disordered state that they fail to warn the victim of an incorrect choice. A forbidden object becomes desirable and commands are met with opposition. This weakness of will is due primarily to the first fall, causing some to find it extremely difficult to differentiate between an apparent and actual good. The vow of obedience provides the radical cure for this infirmity and is one of the main reasons why Christ instituted religious orders. Persons not in religion will obey because necessity forces them to do so, or because the command seems reasonable to them. A religious has no right to consider obedience from the viewpoint of reason; he obeys because he has vowed to do so by sacrificing his will to God. Since rebellion is so deeply rooted in the soul of man it causes him to desire, not always what is best for him but what is in accordance with his wishes at that moment. "There is no merit in obeying when what is commanded seems reasonable to us," was the doctrine of the Little Flower.

St. Thomas teaches: "By the vow of obedience man contracts the obligation of doing for the love of God, what is disagreeable to himself. For this reason he does the things which are most pleasing to God though in themselves they may seem to have little value, because man can offer nothing greater to God than the submission of his will to another man, for no other reason than love of Him."[3]

This is one of the most essential things in religion, a childlike obedience so highly recommended in the Gospel and exemplified in the life of Christ. This virtue is most pleasing to God because it cannot be acquired without a perfect purification of spirit and the perfection of charity. Since no religious practice has any value without obedience than the attainment of perfect submission of heart and will to God is one of the chief aims of religious life.

It is possible to find in religious houses persons who are not completely cured of rebellion of heart. It is even possible that years of religious life have hardened rather than softened their wills. They claim to have no attachment to things which are sinful yet they stubbornly follow their own whims at all times. At times, we also meet souls that are a great enigma to themselves and to those who have to direct them. Although formally they would not break a formal precept of obedience, secretly they take a special delight in mortifying and contradicting the wishes of their superiors. They are fully aware that their actions are displeasing to superiors and may be the cause of disturbance in the community but their repugnance to obedience is greater than their desire of amendment.

How can such troublemakers enjoy peace of conscience? Is it possible that they are not aware, at least vaguely, of the subtle spirit of rebellion which causes them to commit such grievous sins of contempt of authority? Are they unconcerned with the spirit of charity and obedience which should regulate their relationship with their superiors? It is questionable whether or not this inclination of easily violating the command of superiors has not formed in the offenders a habit of repugnance for the practice of obedience. It is evident from the words of St. Thomas Aquinas: "Those who despise law or authority of superiors, or who make the attainment of religious perfection impossible commit a mortal sin."[4]

Superiors, as well as subjects, are not freed from the danger of offending God grievously. Therefore, their only safety lies in humble and simple submission to the rules of their order. It should be remembered, however, that although contempt is possible and easy, it is not always the basis for disobedience. Pride is the chief cause of sins of disobedience, just as it is of all other sins; nevertheless there is almost always some other cause present that lessens the malice of our transgressions. Superiors, then, should strive for the attainment of deep humility.

One of the causes that attenuate the malice of disobedience on the part of subjects will be found in the personal qualities of the superior. Since no person is entirely free from selfishness or sensitiveness, human frailty will find in the supposed defects of the superior a reason which will dispense the subject from obeying his commands promptly and cordially. In such an instance, disobedience is the result, not of formal contempt for authority but of a personal dislike for the person in whom the authority is invested. Such a person reasons thus: "I would be obedient if my superiors were what they should be. Never would I offer resistance to their commands if I were certain that they were prompted by the spirit of rectitude and prudence. Yet it is extremely difficult to obey promptly and blindly those who seem to me destitute of the virtue and talent requisite for their office." This is the state of mind subtly suggested by Satan to those who habitually transgress holy obedience. Their lack of submission to superiors is not due to contempt of authority but to self-deception which considers commands as lacking in prudence and wisdom. Since self-love blinds such victims to the divine Will, their wills refuse to concede to the human invested with divine authority. Such a condition denotes a lamentable state of conscience and does not speak well for the virtue of the subjects. Such an attitude renders the attainment of perfection almost impossible.

Christ instituted the religious life on the basis of the evangelical counsels and in giving these counsels to the multitude He said: "I tell you, that unless your justice abound more than that of the Scribes and Pharisees, you shall not enter into the kingdom of heaven. . . . For if you love them that love you, what reward shall you have? Do not even the publicans this? And if you salute your brethren only, what do you more? Do not even the heathens this? Be you therefore perfect, as also your heavenly Father is perfect.[5] . . . For not everyone that saith to me, Lord, Lord, shall enter into the kingdom of heaven."[6]

These words of our Lord should induce us to reflect very seriously on our motive for leaving the world and entering religious life. This motive should have been explicitly that of fulfilling the evangelical counsels. For precisely this purpose the religious life has been enriched with so many graces and privileges, a fact which affirms the statement that the spirit of submission must be greater among religious than it is among Christians in general. If we obey only exteriorly, without interior submission, then we have no right to any supernatural reward. Even slaves are obedient exteriorly, and the devils must obey God. Our obedience, then, must be more than just submitting our wills to persons or commands naturally pleasing to us. If our obedience is not greater than that of the rest of mankind then we shall indeed fare badly on the day of the final reckoning.

The great St. Theresa says: "Since the devil knows that there is no greater virtue than obedience he will do all in his power to overcome us in this virtue. Obedience means the summit of perfection. No interior recollection, no exterior mortification, no visions nor even the spirit of prophecy will merit us anything in the eyes of God unless our will is completely conformed with His; unless we have learned to temper the bitter with the sweet, accepting all as the will of God."[7]

Therefore obedience without sacrifice is of no value. Any pretext we have for disobedience excuses us but little. This particular admonition relative to obedience is directed primarily toward those who would thus excuse themselves for their continued acts of disobedience. ". . . any obedience will be vain, or will be completely unfruitful, if you take offense at any displeasing characteristic of the superior, and you obey only when you find his commands pleasing and good to yourself."[8] This is indeed a hard saying but unless we heed it we risk the loss of all the merit of our obedience even when we think we have been most virtuous. Moral actions derive their merit from the motive or the intention with which they are performed, and not from their mere execution. That which must be sacrificed on the altar of religious life is our own will. Only by so doing will a religious give to God the honor and glory which is His due. Religious life must be the exact antithesis of the spirit of independence prevalent in the world. Yet this is the only way by which we may arrive at the state of perfect sanctity for as the Holy Spirit says, "True glory is to be found in humiliation."[9]

Our holy Father, St. John, sums it very aptly in these words: ". . . the religious who truly loves God is the religious who has abandoned all things for His sake, because his richness consists in complete abandonment to God, not doing anything for his own glory but solely out of love and resignation to the will of God."[10]

CHAPTER THIRTEEN

THE EUCHARIST AND OBEDIENCE

A study of the superior's qualities merely to regulate our actions, exposes us to the danger of rendering our obedience void of all personal merit. The principle, well known to all who have read anything about asceticism, that the Lord rewards our actions, not on account of their intrinsic value, but for the intention and spirit with which they are performed, should form the basis of religious obedience. It is well, also, to consider the words of our Lord, "Take heed that you do not your justice before men, to be seen by them; otherwise you shall not have a reward of your Father, Who is in heaven . . . when thou dost give alms, let not thy left hand know what thy right hand doth, that thy alms may be in secret, and thy Father, who seeth in secret will repay thee. . . . And when you fast, be not as the hypocrites, sad. For they disfigure their faces, that they may appear unto men to fast. Amen I say unto you they have received their reward. But thou, when thou fastest, anoint thy head and wash thy face, that thou appear not to men to fast, but to thy Father who is in secret; and thy Father, Who seeth in secret will repay thee."[1] "He that receiveth you, receiveth me: and he that receiveth Me, receiveth him that sent Me. . . . And he that receiveth a just man in the name of a just man shall receive the reward of a just man. And whosoever shall give to drink to one of these little ones a cup of cold water only in the name of a disciple, amen, I say to you, he shall not lose his reward."[2]

Therefore those who obey only on account of the good qualities of a superior render their obedience useless since obedience is thus relegated to a purely natural level. The only recompense they will have for their work is the pleasure of pleasing man. St. John says: "Thou hast received thy reward; thou hast obeyed thy superior for his good qualities; and has had no concern in obeying God

80

in him. Thy reward, therefore, must be paid by men and not by God, and that reward you have already received."

When one is continually looking for undesirable qualities in a superior he is bound to find them for it is impossible to appear perfect before those with whom we come in daily contact. This gives rise to rash judgment and with it all the hazards which are mentioned in the third admonition against the world. The consequences in this instance are far more disastrous because they are directed toward one who is the representative of God. The inevitable result is sins of the tongue as well as scandalizing those who hear our uncharitable and irreverent remarks.

Let us also consider an experience which is familiar to nearly everyone. The allusion here is the unfavorable thoughts and murmurings against those whom we may consider superior to ourselves either in social position or talents, or simply because they receive more attention than we do. Some persons of inferior character actually take pleasure in ridiculing the defects of prominent persons. Who has not been guilty at some time or other of this very practice? The basis of such action is a pride which naturally feels humiliated before superior persons. This pride takes extreme delight in exposing any defect which would tend to diminish the good qualities of those who surpass them, while, on the other hand, we tend to minimize the defects of those to whom we are naturally attracted. To acknowledge this weakness of the human heart is the first step toward its correction. That a person is in religious life does not entirely exempt him from this weakness and he must therefore keep a constant guard lest he fall into lamentable disorders.

The aim of religious life is to attain the spirit of prompt and simple submission to the will of God as manifested by the rule or the superior. This virtue, which is the most delicate flower of charity, induces God to take great delight in the soul that possesses it; yet it is precisely so delicate that a single murmur against the superior who makes known to us the will of God can bring about its destruction. No poison injected into the veins reacts more rapidly nor with more deadly effects than murmuring against commands. It awakens quickly and strongly the spirit of pride and secret rebellion which we all have lurking in the innermost recesses of our heart. It was in this manner that the devil tempted Eve. Our first parents knew great happiness in their simple obedience to the will of God and it required only a little murmuring by the enemy against God to make them believe that God was jealous lest they become like to Himself, knowing good and evil. "He has forbidden you," said the crafty serpent, "Because God doth know that in what day so ever you shall eat thereof, your eyes shall be opened; and you shall be as Gods, knowing good and evil."[3]

Thus through fatal and calumnious murmuring against God, the first and most disastrous disobedience came into the world. It is certain that nearly all sins which have followed, and will follow until the end of time, have as their proximate cause some internal or external murmuring against the person of a superior. Those engaged in spreading the faults of a superior are guilty of scandal, a sin against which our Lord was inexorable. "Woe to him through whom [scandal] comes. It were better for him that a millstone were hanged about his neck, and he cast into the sea, than that he should scandalize one of these little ones."[4]

Just as scandal and murmuring cause great havoc in the world, so too, it causes even greater damage in religious life. The greatest good and the final end of religious life is charity radiated through a spirit of simple submission; and for one to be guilty of causing other souls to lose their confidence in a superior is an evil, the gravity of which is in proportion to the damage entailed. It is little wonder, then, that St. John says that to fix our attention on the defects of the superior will bring about the ruination of religious perfection and will prevent religious from keeping their vows. He who pays no attention to the person who commands, but rather to what is commanded will be freed from this evil for he realizes thoroughly that the superior takes the place of God.

If all superiors were angels instead of men, then religious would fulfill their commands without question. Since this premise is not true and superiors may be mistaken in their given commands the objection is sometimes raised that obedience cannot bind when the command seems unreasonable or nonsensical. St. John commands perfect submission but he does not ask us to renounce our reason, even when we obey. "Listen with reason performing your actions in accordance with the will of God and this will benefit you more than all good works done heedlessly. Blessed is he, who, setting his own tastes and inclinations aside, looks at things according to reason and justice in order to accomplish them more perfectly."[5]

The same right reason tells us that we must obey the superior at all times with the exception of the following cases: the order is unjust, or contrary to natural law, the law of God, or of the church; or a serious matter is involved. In each instance it is clear that it would be unreasonable to obey such a command. Such orders, however, prove to be the exception to the ordinary commands of obedience and since this is true we must make certain that we are not misguided by our self-will or self-love when a command not to our liking is given. The fact that we think that the superior's orders are not prudent, or that we know a better method of execution than the one prescribed should never dispense with the obligation of accepting them unless there is definite evidence of error on the part of the superior. To act contrary to this would render both religious and social life impossible and authority nothing but a ridiculous figure.

The superior has to consider the command from the supernatural viewpoint, as best suited for the common good, and in complete accordance with the spirit of the law. On the other hand, no subject is completely cognizant of the circumstances involved in the superior's action. It is not enough to recognize the ideal good, or what is perfect and beautiful because this in itself is not eminently practical. It is necessary to know the "here and now," or relatively speaking to consider first all the circumstances related to the ideal good. There is much truth in the saying "The best is the enemy of the good." St. Francis de Sales said with much wit and saintly malice: "There are men who, by dint of persistence in living like angels, forget to conduct themselves as men."[6]

The fact that human nature is intricate and complicated must be taken into consideration, therefore a command should not be contrary to human reason. When it is not, then conscience tells us that we must accept with submission whatever orders may be given by any superior when it is evident that it is not contrary to the law of God or of the Church. In religious life there are several acts which are in themselves indifferent and can be performed in thousands of ways with no detriment, whatsoever, to religious spirit. Yet it is these very small matters of everyday life that often serve as the cobwebs entangling religious in uncertainty. The gift of a good ruler, in this case, would consist in keeping his subjects from becoming entangled in such webs. On the part of the subject it may be that the origin of these petty offenses lies in the strange attitude that the superior is taking special delight in provoking a person to minute obligations of the rule. Although occasionally it may be expedient to test a particular religious in order to sanctify him, it would be sheer madness to follow such a course as a general rule. Since superiors are human beings too, it may be that however prudent they may be, they jar the sensibilities of their subjects at times by their commands. In this case, the best course to be followed by the subject is one of blind obedience accompanied by a decided effort to overcome his feelings. If the superior should be at fault, then an opportune remark made with good will and respect may often prove more pleasing to God and more beneficial to a religious house than costly obedience. Such an action presupposes great charity on the part of the person who undertakes it.

The spirit of talebearing and carrying stories to a superior is mean and detestable. To entertain any resentment, however small, and above all to carry it from tongue to tongue is both vile and dangerous. A person who feels such resentment must try to overcome it with sincere acts of obedience and love of God. Such talebearing may be the cause of superiors mortifying their subjects without their consciously realizing it. This, of course, does not refer to a religious who prudently and humbly makes a justifiable remark which will result in much good. It must be understood, however, that such a remark is not an admonition and while the maker of the remark has the right to grateful recognition it is not necessary that the superior act on the information which he has received. To reason contrary to this would mean that the subject is supplanting the superior's judgment with his own and this is always the ruination of authority. It is to be remembered that the superior may have many reasons unknown to the individual for keeping his own point of view and it is not necessary to reveal this knowledge.

The genuine religious spirit consists in immediately expelling any insinuations Satan might make concerning the inability of the person who is giving the command. A true religious does not stop to consider whether what he has been commanded is expedient or not. It is both the spirit and the letter of our rule: "That you may not be judged for contempt but may merit rather eternal reward for your obedience." This is reiterated by St. John in the admonition: "Bear in mind what has been said concerning the superior and you will profit greatly. Otherwise you may come to great harm."

The life and the example of the saints should act as a stimulus for us for there never was a saint who was not obedient. Above all we have the perfect model of obedience, our divine Redeemer, who came not to do His own will but the will of His Father. He who with one hand sustains the world and on whom all creatures depend, wished as man to depend on a most delicate Virgin and a poor artisan. All that He did in His adorable infancy and youth, the holy Gospel comprises in words: "He was subject to them."[7] He accepted His bitter passion and death in the Garden of Olives saying, "Not My will but Thine be done."[8] Finally the consummation of His earthly obedience was His surrender of Himself into the hands of His executioners, protesting that He did so to fulfill the will of His heavenly Father.

But the most admirable example of obedience is not found in His mortal life but rather in His life in the Holy Eucharist. Here His obedience is fathomless. Through the sacred Mass and Holy Communion we religious come into intimate, daily contact with the adorable Heart of the Savior. Having received Him we hold within our hearts the Son of God; He who was subject to Mary and Joseph; who in Judea caressed the little children, healed the sick, and raised the dead; who said to all: "If any man will come after me, let him deny himself, and take up his cross daily, and follow Me."[9] On the day of our religious profession we accepted this promise choosing continuous obedience as our principal cross, and joyfully we heard His words, "I have given you an example, . . . so you do also."[10] The greatest example He gave was that of perfect and unquestioning obedience. Perhaps we may object in our weakness that since He was the Son of God, it was a pleasure and easy to obey Mary and Joseph. Yet, although these were two pre-eminently holy creatures, He was their creator. But His obedience goes even farther than this for His greatest pleasure today is found in His continued perfect obedience in the Holy Eucharist to all priests, the good and the bad, the worthy and the unworthy.

Whatever temptation against obedience a religious faces he can find the answer and the cure in simple, humble meditation before the Blessed Sacrament. If at times obedience is irksome because of the discordant characteristics of the superior, let us kneel before the tabernacle whence Jesus will speak to our soul: "My child, do not complain; do not be disturbed. Learn absolute subjection, and silence from me. Do the characteristics of your superior displease you, my poor child? Do you think that all who handle me in the Eucharist are pleasing to me? What would become of the world if in this Sacrament I obeyed good priests only? How few souls would enjoy My presence if I allowed Myself to be united only with worthy and pure souls? Are you not willing to endure even a little for Me, whom you promised to follow and to whom you have protested your undying love? Rise, o ye of little faith and joyfully take up your cross, which will secure for you an everlasting reward. Obey, suffer, and be silent according to the example I am giving you in the Eucharist. Will you not love Me, even as I have loved you?"

Here in the tabernacle we find the perfect ideal of the religious life. We find the divine Exemplar of perfect obedience, complete abnegation, silence, and sacrifice. Happy the soul who frequently and especially in critical moments comes to this august school to learn the lessons of fortitude. It is here that you will be strengthened with the grace of God and the perseverance necessary to obey always. Then all the austerities of religious life will become easy. You will be freed from the deceits of the enemy, and all of your actions, even the most menial, will merit a most exalted glory in heaven.

CHAPTER FOURTEEN

HUMILITY

The third admonition against the devil is ". . . to humble thy heart in word and deed, rejoicing more at another's good than at thine own; desiring that others be preferred to yourself in all things, and this particularly in respect to those who attract you the least. In this way thou shalt overcome evil with good and cast the devil far from thee. If you fail to do this, you will never attain true charity."[1]

Apparently this admonition requires no commentary, inasmuch as its text is plain enough and the subject matter is well known, not only to religious but also to anyone familiar with religious treatises. Moreover, so much has been written on humility and on its opposing vice, that it would be foolish to pretend to write anything new. Despite this fact, however, it may be well to make a further study of this admonition, for often what is most familiar is the least understood.

Ascetic and pious books frequently use the word *humility* and yet perhaps there is no word more commonly misinterpreted. It is the belief of some devout souls, as well as some educators, that humility is merely a constant effort to suppress all thoughts and words favorable to themselves, regardless of what the truth of the situation may be. Every human being has some particular talent, yet this misrepresentation of humility refuses to recognize either native ability or accomplishment. Thus, we find persons speaking most abjectly of themselves while interiorly they think the exact opposite. This is nothing more than making the virtue which is most dear to the Lord's heart, an act of hypocrisy. Not content with deceiving themselves, these people impose their theory and misunderstanding on other unsuspecting souls. A clear example of this type of so-called humility is found in the story of a good man, but a poor educator, who criticized a literary work of a subordinate. His criticism was unjust and severe, despite the fact that the work had received public acclamation. After having humiliated his subject, the critic, satisfied that he had accomplished a worthy task, said, "Young people must be treated harshly in order to keep their spirit of humility." Such a pharisaical and exaggerated idea of humility, as well as the disastrous method of inculcating it, is most certainly not genuine humility as it is understood by the saints.

The teachings of the great masters of Carmel, St. John of the Cross and St. Theresa, are identical on this point. To St. John, humility is the first fruit of love and light; and to St. Theresa, it is truth. The origin and nature of humility is fully explained by St. John: "When one has reached the third degree of love of God, he considers great works undertaken for the Beloved as nothing; many things are accomplished as nothing, and the long time wherein he serves Him is relatively short. Because of the fire of love which consumes it the soul considers great pain and afflictions as trifles; and if it were lawful for it to be destroyed a thousand times for His glory, it would be comforted. It considers all that is not done for God as useless, and at the same time, considers itself as being most inferior to other souls: first, because love is continually teaching it how much is due to God and secondly, because it realizes that these works are faulty and imperfect. This covers the soul with confusion because it realizes how incomparable are his works to the omnipotent God. A soul which has reached this third degree of humility is far from vainglory or presumption since it realizes its complete dependence on God."[2]

From this beautiful passage of the Mystical Doctor we can formulate two principles: first, that a soul burning with great love looks upon all it does as unprofitable. Second, as love continues to show the debt due to God it recognizes all its works as unworthy of such a Master. This is the natural effect of perfect love, for what true lover has ever been satisfied until he has given his very life for the object of his love? Nobody can love, or even understand what love is, if he is incapable of comprehending that it is happiness and pleasure for the lover to die for the object of his love. Every person gifted with a noble heart and mind knows this profound proverb: "Love knows no limits, and never says 'enough.'" Still less will it say "enough" when the object is God, for God is infinite love. It is also clear that the more a man loves God, the better he knows Him; and the more he knows God the better he will understand what His infinite sanctity, eternal power, immense goodness, and inexhaustible mercy require from His creatures. Then turning his eyes upon himself he finds that his works which may seem good to others are deficient and lacking in the sight of God. Feelings of contempt for himself and his own works spring from this perfect love and clear knowledge of God. These true sentiments create the genuine spirit of humility. To understand these sentiments and to be convinced of living according to these convictions is to be truly humble of heart and mind. Any other use of the word *humility* is a source of deception to one's self and to others.

Humility, then, according to St. John, is the fruit of that degree of divine love which cannot be satisfied with the little that man is able to do for God. It is a result of that light which permits us to have a glimpse of what God is and what we are in comparison. It shows us to some extent, what He deserves and how infinitesimal are our works in comparison with His greatness.

The teaching of St. Theresa on humility agrees perfectly with that of her disciple and master. While her doctrine may not be so profound and methodical yet it is explained in her own charming fashion: "I was wondering once why our Lord so dearly loved the virtue of humility; when suddenly the following reason came to my mind. God is sovereign truth and to be humble is to walk in truth, for it is absolutely true that of ourselves we have only misery and nothingness; anyone who fails to understand this is walking in falsehood. He who best understands is most pleasing to sovereign truth because he is walking on the path of truth."[3]

Before commenting on this passage let us consider a less familiar one that complements the aforesaid: "A soul having a high degree of love clearly sees its own wretchedness, for in a room bathed in sunlight, not a cobweb can remain hidden. . . . It can never be guilty of vainglory realizing fully that of itself it can do little or nothing. . . . The soul realizes that it has merited hell because of its actions, but that it is promised heaven because of infinite Love."[4]

St. Theresa insists that the basis of true humility is a well-founded truth. There is no false humility or asceticism in this doctrine because the humility is dependent on and proportionate to the light the soul receives. The more light the soul receives the more clearly it will see its own weaknesses and defects, and the more reason it has to humble itself profoundly before God.

Most individuals are aware that they are filled with defects but since these ideas are not too clear nor definite then they exercise but a minor influence on their lives. It is certain that the clearer our understanding and the more fixed and penetrating our look toward the interior of our soul the greater and more varied will be the imperfections which we find in ourselves. It is through the light of grace that these faults are detected for according to the beautiful phrase of St. Theresa ". . . in a room bathed in sunlight, not a cobweb can remain hidden."

True humility does not ask us to recognize the fact that we are a mixture of good and bad, nor that supernatural life has endowed us with magnificent qualities of grace. St. Theresa's doctrine relative to this is admirable: "Humility is the realization that what we possess is ours only because it has been given to us by God. Let us understand thoroughly that these gifts are not the reward of our own merits, but rather an expression of the great love that God has for us. Unless we recognize all things as coming from God then we shall not be moved to love Him. Once we have assured ourselves that of ourselves we are nothing, then we become immeasurably rich. This is what is meant by genuine humility, and its practice constrains us to love God more ardently. The prayer founded on humility seeks new strength to serve God with a greater love and gratitude, thus the talents which are given are but exchanged for greater ones in the eyes of God. If this is not the type of humility we strive for then God will withdraw His grace and we shall find ourselves poorer than before, because the very graces meant to be ours will be given to those who can profit by them and increase them."[5]

According to this teaching, true humility considers us as we are, presupposing sufficient correspondence with the light given to evaluate ourselves as we are in the eyes of God. We not only discover our deficiencies but we recognize and appreciate whatever good qualities we may possess in the physical, moral, natural, or supernatural order. The recognition is twofold, first a dependence upon God as the Author of these gifts, and second a realization of the responsibility entailed in these talents given to us. Finally, there is

the realization that these treasures are contained in fragile vessels
that can be easily despoiled on the dangerous road to perfection.
All these thoughts are expressed in the apparently simple but profound words of St. Theresa, "Humility is walking in truth."

It is evident that St. Theresa considered humility as the legitimate
daughter of truth, just as St. John considered it the genuine
daughter of love, yet the two are equivalent because the fruit of
humility is love. The natural effect produced in the mind and
heart of man by humility is the perfect knowledge of God and of
himself and the corresponding relationship between them. It would
be difficult, then, to find a more beautiful or more exact definition
of humility than "Humility is walking in truth." It is well to understand clearly the full import of this truth because there is nothing
more dangerous than a partially understood truth. Absolute falsehood would be rejected immediately but a half-truth becomes proportionately dangerous, relative to the importance of the truth that
it tries to resemble.

Understanding that humility is truth, puts to flight the false
humility of the ignorant as well as the deceits of the insincere.
Those who only wish to satisfy their ostentation and vanity are
not equipped to understand or to practice the humility of St.
Theresa. They are so anxious to win the admiration of those around
them that they forget to direct the credit where it belongs. The
talents they possess are not of their own merits but rather a free
gift from God, therefore the glory of these talents belongs to God.

If anyone really possesses great qualities and talents, humility
does not require him to deny them. Surely, St. Thomas Aquinas,
wise and humble as he was, would not claim that his knowledge
of philosophy and theology was less than that of the cook in his
monastery. What humility does require of us is that we appreciate
the gifts that God has given us, that we make good use of them
for the glory of God and the benefit of our neighbor. To be truly
humble we must bear in mind the following principles: Self-love
naturally enlarges and exaggerates our perfections while it mini-
mizes our defects, therefore it is very easy to deceive oneself in
this regard. A perfect understanding of our talents and acting
accordingly is walking in truth; it is being perfectly humble. Second,
whatever good qualities or talents we possess must be held as a
sacred trust given to us by God, for which we must render an

account on the final day. This we know from the parable of the slothful servant who wasted his talent.[6] Each gift, then, bears with it a corresponding responsibility. The prudent and wise endeavor to render a good account of their talents, whereas the foolish and slothful squander the little they have received. Again, this is walking in truth. Finally God wishes to find among men the same harmony and dependence which we find in the physical world around us. God loves all of His creatures; therefore He commands us to love one another as children of the same Father, and to do unto others as we would wish them to do unto us.[7] Whatever gifts God has passed on to us, have been given for the purpose of helping our neighbor. "Let no man, therefore, glory in men. For all things are yours, whether it be Paul, . . . or Cephas, or the world, . . . or things present, or things to come — for all are yours; and you are Christ's and Christ is God's."[8] "Freely you have received, freely give,"[9] says our divine Redeemer, and St. Paul adds: "I endure all things for the sake of the elect."[10]

Everything God does as well as everything He gives is for a definite purpose; hence, the more talents we possess the greater our obligations toward our neighbors. This is what Christ referred to when He said, "When you shall have done all these things that are commanded you, say: 'We are unprofitable servants; we have done that which we ought to do.'"[11] A perfect understanding of this is to walk in truth.

The spirit of humility, then, according to the spirit of both St. Theresa and St. John, contains no vanity, no ostentation, no repulsiveness. It is filled with sincerity and spreads abroad the fire of charity. Man, instead of trying to glorify himself, is solicitous for the glory of God and the benefit of his neighbor; and instead of using his talents for himself they are used to bring men closer to God, the source of true humility.

In her Way of Perfection St. Theresa says that all religious perfection consists in three things: "Love for each other; detachment from all created things; and true humility. That which comes last is the most important, and when practiced faithfully embraces all the rest."[12]

CHAPTER FIFTEEN

ENVY

Although the fourth and fifth admonitions suggest methods of opposition to the devil, St. John especially recommends humility as the most direct method of overcoming his insidious attacks and wiles. Humility is inseparable from truth, and our Lord warns us that the devil, filled with deceit, is the enemy of truth. "For he is a liar and the father thereof."[1] Truth presupposes a certain disregard for self accompanied by the love of God, which love will increase in proportion to the growth of humility. St. John says of such a soul, closely united to God, "When the greatest extreme of humility has reduced a man to mere nothingness, then a complete union is wrought between the soul and God."[2] This is in direct antithesis to the teachings of Satan who is utterly incapable of loving God or any of His creatures. "So intense is his hatred, even for other devils like unto himself, that he would completely destroy them and in so doing annihilate the glory of God, as well as His love, if such were possible."[3] On the contrary, the humble, forgetting themselves, rejoice in the glory of God and the good of their neighbor striving with all their might to promote the common welfare and the divine glory. True humility is nourished by filial affection for God, strengthened by the example of Christ, and deepened by the Mystery of the Redemption.

Directly opposed to humility is the spirit of Satan who "as a roaring lion, goeth about seeking whom he may devour"[4] and taking great pleasure in inciting his victims to two predominant sins, pride and jealousy. These two sins are sufficient to serve his purposes, because they completely undermine the two chief effects of humility, love of God and love of neighbor.

The evil spirit sinned by coveting the excellence which is singular to God alone. This intellectual pride caused him who had been known as the "Prince of light" to become the "Prince of darkness."

No sooner was he overcome by pride than he was filled with envy which caused him to grieve over the divine excellence and the power of man to share in the glory of God.

Sacred Scripture always depicts the humble as being the dearest to the heart of God: "The Lord is high above all nations; and His glory above the heavens. Who is as the Lord our God, Who dwelleth on high; and looketh down on the low things in heaven and in earth?"[5] "The Almighty and Omnipotent who possesses eternity dwelleth with the contrite and humble spirit,"[6] says Isaias, who further adds: "This saith the Lord: 'Heaven is my throne, and the earth my footstool . . . to whom shall I have respect, but to him that is poor and . . . of a contrite heart?'"[7] David assures us that the Lord never rejects the contrite and humble of heart, and God Himself reveals that He spoke intimately to Moses, his servant, "I speak to him . . . plainly, and not by . . . figures doth he see the Lord."[8] Sacred Scripture has a further reference to this when it remarks: "Moses was a man exceedingly meek above all men that dwelt upon earth."[9]

According to the sages of the Old Testament humility is the foundation of all solid and durable greatness: "The greater thou art, the more humble thyself in all things, and thou shalt find grace before God; for great is the power of God alone, and He is honored by the humble."[10] Since only the humble of heart may enter into heaven, then humility must precede glory. When the Apostles asked our divine Lord who would be the greater in the kingdom of God, He took a child and set him in the midst of them, saying, "Whosoever shall humble himself as this little child, he is the greater in the kingdom of heaven.[11] . . . Whosoever shall exalt himself shall be humbled; and he that shall humble himself shall be exalted."[12]

Regardless of the number of times we have heard these words of our divine Savior, we still find it difficult to make them the guiding principle of our life! Yet Holy Scripture is filled with passages eulogizing humility and meekness.

Christ, knowing well the cost of humility, set a powerful example counseling all those who would be His followers: "Learn of Me, because I am meek and humble of heart: and you shall find rest to your souls."[13] How well He understood the excessive jealousy with which each man guards his honor and personal dignity. How well He knew the innate ambition of all men to seek the first and highest place for himself. It was precisely to curb this predominant yearning that the meek and lowly Master stated His doctrine: "The disciple is not above the Master, nor the servant above his lord. . . . You call Me master and Lord and you say well, for so I am."[14] Learn of Me, not my infinite wisdom, not the power to subject demons, not the power to raise the dead to life, nor to command the elements, but rather learn the humility and meekness of My Heart. "I have given you an example, that as I have done to you, so you do also. . . . If you know these things, you shall be blessed if you do them."[15] The entire doctrine of Christ was a canticle of meekness and humility which was perfectly reflected in all His sermons and actions.

It is evident that the more pleasing humility is in the eyes of God the more hateful must be the contrary vice of pride. There are several instances of the insolence and pride of rulers, as well as the lowly, which met with corresponding humiliations. King Antiochus is a perfect model of pride, thinking that he possessed the power to command and restrict the elements. Yet in the height of his power he was stricken by the Lord and brought to complete dependence upon the menials of his court.

Another instance of this pride was Sennacherib who threatened the chosen people with complete destruction, claiming that he had completely destroyed and stripped the forests of Libanus. But the Lord sent him this message by the Prophet Isaias: "Thy very pride has deceived thee . . . but though thou shouldst make thy nest as high as an eagle's, I will bring thee down from thence, saith the Lord, God and you shall be brought low, and I will turn thee back by the very road that thou hast traveled."[16]

It is evident that our Lord cannot tolerate those who are haughty and proud, who act as if all goodness they possess comes from their own merits; these He turns from as from a loathsome object. Since God is infinite justice and goodness, He takes great pleasure in communicating His pleasures and riches to those who are best disposed to receive them. But He cannot give His glory to those who consider themselves greater than He; for if He were to be deprived of this glory, then He would cease to be God. It is not strange that pride is so repugnant to the Lord since He has offered an outstanding example of humility in all things. The sin

of pride consists in a desire of appropriating the glory which is due
to God and since this is so God can do nothing but despise those
who wish to deprive Him of what is justly His. This explains
why arrogance and pride in this life are so frequently followed
by bitter deceptions and humiliating misfortunes; while genuine
humility is followed by legitimate glory and genuine esteem.
"Where pride is, there also shall be reproach,"[17] says Solomon,
and David adds, "I have seen the wicked highly exalted, and lifted
up like the cedars of Libanus; and I passed by, and lo, he was not;
and I sought him and his place was not found."[18]

Pride, the first capital sin, has most deeply corrupted human
nature and caused the greatest ruination to souls. In its final
analysis, it is nothing more than the perversion of universal evil.
Did God not create man to be king? Did He not say to our
first parents: "Fill the earth, and subdue it, and rule over the
fishes of the sea, and the fowls of the air."[19] This command in-
cluded the spirit of ambition, the insatiable craving of never being
fully satisfied with what we would possess here on earth.

Pride is self-love inordinately seeking its own superiority. Yet
self-love is not evil in its origin because God, Himself, placed it
in the human heart; nor is it evil in its seeking superiority, because
God has not created us for infamy but rather for glory. "Our confidence is such," says St. Paul, "that we do not fear the dissolution
of the body in order to fully possess God."[20] Christ verified this
statement at the last supper when He said, "Father, I will that
where I am, they also whom thou hast given me may be."[21]

The evil of self-love does not consist in man's loving himself
nor in seeking to improve; rather it is to be found in the means
employed to achieve this end. "Man cannot love that which is
contrary to his nature. Therefore, the desire to excel, either in
the natural or supernatural order, is not in itself sinful, unless
contrary means are used to obtain the end. The sin of pride lies
precisely in the lack of subjection to what is its superior."[22]

Our first parents did not sin by wishing to be like God, for they
had been made to the image and likeness of God; rather they
desired the superior prerogative of excellence which was not lawfully theirs. When we commit a sin of pride it is not merely that
we esteem our own superiority but rather that we pretend to
acquire it by improper means. Excellence is not to be found in self

but in God alone. "Let him who takes pride, take pride in the Lord,"[23] never in men. The only road to sublime excellence is the faithful observance of the law in the spirit of humility and meekness; "If thou wilt enter into life, keep the commandments. . . . Amen, I say unto you, unless you be converted and become as little children, you shall not enter into the kingdom of heaven."[24] This is the clear and positive statement of Christ, who can neither deceive nor be deceived. Any other interpretations are self-deception.

This is also the teaching of St. John of the Cross: "When God loves a soul, He does not regard its superior qualities, but rather the greatness of its self-contempt and humility."[25]

It follows, then, that the more one acknowledges himself as nothing before God, the more he will be exalted. Why should man exalt himself? If he possesses any good, did it not come from God? The great St. Paul says: "What hast thou that thou has not received? And if thou hast received, why dost thou glory, as if thou hadst not received it?"[26] This doctrine is identical with that of St. John: "If you desire self-glory, what have you that is your own? There remains nothingness, and in this should be your glory."[27]

One of the worst and most repugnant features of pride is its inseparable companion, envy. It is natural for the proud to feel sadness when they see others possessing and enjoying what they so ardently desire but cannot have. This unhappiness and loathing over the welfare of our neighbor is envy, the most despicable of all vices found in the human soul with the exception of pride. It is contrary to the highest and noblest emotions of human friendships which naturally delights in the welfare of others. Feelings of envy cause the greatest havoc, killing noble and delicate sentiments, embittering the purest and holiest pleasures, and rendering intolerable the peace and contentment meant to be the lot of the children of God.

Envy is the daughter of pride and the twin sister of jealousy. It desires the exaltation of self alone; and when it fails, it despises all and becomes despised. It hates and becomes hateful. Pride would have all honor and happiness for itself alone, but contrariwise it nearly always reaps dislike and humiliation. For this reason it takes unusual pleasure in defaming the honor of the neighbor and destroying the peace and happiness he enjoys. Pride and envy are fomented and fostered by the evil spirit from whom they originally proceeded. The devil, having lost eternity himself, envies and despises those who are destined for the glory which he repudiated and rejoices when he can prevent someone from attaining eternity. Since he cannot love, he takes singular pleasure in causing others to hate. Just as a snake injects its poison into all who approach it, so the evil spirit injects envy into the hearts of men. Holy Scripture says, "Envy is the rottenness of the bones."[28] As corruption destroys the vital tissues of the body and torments the victim, likewise envy torments and destroys the heart and mind of the envious. Envy is so despicable and subtle that it can attack even the most unsuspecting. Just as the snake winds through the most beautiful gardens, so envy lurks in the shadow of innocent hearts and disturbs the peace of those who walk along the paths of virtue and honor.

To counteract the poison of envy it is well to bear in mind the words of St. John, "If you desire self-glory, consider thy nothingness and this shall be your glory."[29]

CHAPTER SIXTEEN

SELF-LOVE

The effects of pride on the soul are both many and lamentable. They cannot be more strongly and profoundly expressed than in Holy Scripture: "As wine deceives him who drinks it, so shall the proud man be."[1] "Wine was created from the beginning to make men joyful, not to make them drunk. Wine drunken with moderation is the joy of the soul and the heart."[2] It is healthful for it strengthens the nerves, quickens the imagination, and is a powerful stimulant of all the vital forces. But when it is taken to excess then it renders man disorderly and darkens his mind. An excellent comparison can be made between the foregoing and pride. Pride in moderation is good, but when it becomes excessive it is a perversion of self-love because man takes exclusive complacency in his own excellence.

God has not created any man to hate himself. The instinct of self-love was infused into the soul just as surely as was the instinct of self-preservation. Of itself, self-love is meant to aid the acquisition of virtue and is the necessary stimulant of public and private morality. Without a desire and eagerness for his perfection and glory, man is little more than irrational animals and his aspirations are reduced to a merely sensual level. Hope, honor, and glory would then become meaningless. Without the sentiment of honor and self-esteem, no action would be dishonorable, no vice degrading, and the most delicate virtues become a farce. God has not created man to despise himself absolutely, nor to make himself an object of complete abjection. "You are gods and all of you the sons of the Most High."[3] What more beautiful words could express our need for regulated self-love?

Nobody ever had a higher appreciation of human dignity than the saints, and they were the most humble of men because they understood these words: "Our Father who art in Heaven." We, who are still traveling this road need personal effort assisted by divine grace to achieve our goal. Once we esteem ourselves as children of God then we must act accordingly, and self-love becomes a necessity. If we were to entertain only feelings of absolute abjection and contempt of ourselves we would scarcely make any effort to fulfill our duties in the hope of enjoying the beatific vision.

Humility does not mean that man should renounce entirely every sentiment of honor and excellence, because this would lead to spiritual degradation. No one was better aware of the fact that the sole means of acquiring true honor and glory was true and sincere humility than the saints. Persistent attempts to destroy self-love is an illusion because it is contrary to nature itself. It would simply result in counterfeit virtue which would be odious and impracticable. The regulation of self-love requires great strength of character and a native ability to understand truths correctly and fully. Unless a person can trace the roots of self-love into the inner recesses of his own heart and soul, where it conceals itself so subtly, he will never know how to guide and govern others because his own self-love will run rampant causing innumerable disorders.

Such a person will be guilty of vanity, which is a slight deviation from self-love. There is a striking resemblance between the vain and the semi-intoxicated. Both are generally as joyful as they are inoffensive; and both are inclined to lavish favors on those in need. They do not despise others nor do they entertain ill will toward anyone. They are satisfied with themselves and experience an intimate satisfaction when others feel happy, provided that their own admirable qualities are recognized. The vain, therefore, provoke compassion and pity rather than indignation or contempt. The excessive desire for praise and the fear of being unjustly criticized are both the children of vanity and pride.

However, vanity is not the greatest delusion of self-love. Unrestrained vanity will soon lead to the vice of pride. Vanity is the nurse and mother of pride which is the final evolution of self-love. Contradiction and deception can kill vanity, but if the heart and mind where this vanity originated do not accept these, then pride will rise on its ruins. Thus the second state will be incomparably worse than the first. The proud man is occupied only with himself.

He wants everything and everyone to serve his purpose; he disdains everything else. Nothing is of interest to him unless it contributes to his own satisfaction. The highest expression of the intoxication of pride was displayed by the devil when he offered the kingdoms of the earth to the Son of God: "All these will I give thee, if falling down thou wilt adore me."[4] St. Thomas acclaims the devil as the first principle of pride. Since he is incapable of repentance his many disgraceful losses serve only to increase his pride and suffering leaving in their wake hatred and bitterness. The deeper pride roots and grows in the spirit, the more it will encounter contradiction and unhappiness.

Something very similar to this happens to man. He is first the victim of wounded self-love which results in vanity. Mere contradictions will not serve to cure him because in his own consciousness he fails to recognize and admit his guilt. Unless humiliations are recognized and accepted by our conscience our weakness is not cured because truth and acknowledgment of truth are missing. External humiliations only serve to increase vanity. At times it is expedient and even necessary to humble the haughty but unless this is done with discretion then disastrous results occur. Self-love is within the spirit; therefore the remedy must come from within: "First make clean the inside of the cup and of the dish, that the outside may become clean."[5] While a man remains in the state of vanity he is like a spoiled child, carrying his heart on his sleeve, not to expose his sacrifices, but for the sole purpose of receiving praise and commendation from others. There is not much malice in his actions, neither is there much virtue. Human nature being what it is does not tolerate such vanity for any length of time so it is not long before the vain person is receiving slights instead of attentions; blame in place of praise, and reproaches instead of the fancied satisfaction of esteem and love. If he does not withdraw within himself and accept his own weakness before the tribunal of his own conscience, then he turns against those who have wounded his feelings and he passes from vanity to pride. What he fails to realize is that if vanity was unable to satisfy his longings for esteem and love, much less will this be accomplished by pride. The more he is contradicted the more wounded his self-love becomes and the greater becomes his aversion toward those who humiliate him. It is extremely necessary, then, to avoid this vicious circle of self-love becoming vanity and from thence passing into pride by properly educating and understanding the beginnings of inordinate self-love. This is confirmed by Holy Scripture in the assertion: "The pride of them that hate thee continually increases."[6] The proud are like the intoxicated, the more they drink the thirstier they become; the more they satiate their desires the deeper they sink into degradation. The prophet Habacuc illucidates this comparison: "So shall the proud man be, and he shall not be honored; who hath enlarged his desire . . . and is himself like death, and he is never satisfied."[7]

Notwithstanding the repulsiveness that pride presents it is easily the most common vice in the world. No other vice is so deeply rooted within us and we can all exclaim with Solomon, "Who can say, my heart is clean; I am pure from all sin?"[8] In the moral order the forms and expressions of pride are many and varied. Its intensity ranges from almost unconscious movements of self-complacency, which surprise even those engaged in the best works of piety, to perfect pride which is displayed in a stubborn persistence for evil and a hatred for all that contradicts it. Although humility and pride are in direct antipathy to each other, pride uses everything at its disposal, including talent and virtue. Pride is as common in the cloister as it is in any social circle, attacking persons whose judgment is clear in all matters except those in which self-love intervenes. Self-love clouds their reason and, influenced by emotion, they bitterly assail those who are opposed to their opinions, considering all who do not agree with them culpably ignorant.

Since this type of person is common, the reaction is that such a state is both incurable and intractable; therefore people think it necessary to yield to his whims, not because truth or justice is on his side but because he is selfish and will accept no other decision. Such a victim of pride may even take complacency in such a dishonorable and humiliating concession. Pride is therefore justly styled the intoxication of the spirit. "So wine drunk to excess shall rebuke the hearts of the proud."[9]

Pride does not spare any condition or state of life and its greatest danger lies in the fact that the person afflicted is unaware of his condition. Its victims would be overwhelmed if they could realize that their actions were inspired and animated by a secret pride, lurking in the innermost recesses of their hearts. St. John ascertains that even persons favored with supernatural graces readily fall prey to this ugly vice and he gives these admonitions to recognize the symptoms. "Those filled with aversion and antagonism toward others who fail to recognize their degree of spirituality, their spirit of mortification, or the greatness of their actions are filled with self-esteem and pride which they completely fail to recognize. Outwardly they depreciate their spirituality and lament its weakness, while inwardly they are congratulating themselves that their spiritual gifts surpass those of others. They are like the Pharisee who gave thanks to God that he was not as the rest of men. Although their words may not be identical with those of the Pharisee they habitually resemble him in spirit. Thus the spirit of pride grows to the extent wherein it equals that of Satan himself. To avoid such an evil two things must be considered. First, that virtue does not consist in emotions, however sublime they may be, but rather in humility and deep contempt for oneself. . . . Second, virtue does not consist in visions nor revelations but in the minutest act of humility. The truly humble person does not esteem himself, nor think evil of others, but considers himself as he truly is in the eyes of God."[10]

From this we may conclude that pride, vanity, and jealousy are nothing more than so many degrees or manifestations of misunderstood and ineffectually guided self-love. Very few souls are completely exempted from these weaknesses, therefore we must be on the alert to detect their earliest signs. Since the cause is interior, outward violence is not the cure; the opposition must be interior and our conscience must be actuated by interior light and truth which can come only from humble and persevering prayer. The truth, well meditated on, brings knowledge of the greatness of our misery compared to the omnipotence of God; of the lowliness of our present condition and the loftiness of our destiny; of how humility embellishes the soul and makes it lovable in the sight of God and men; and of how pride deforms and torments the soul making it hateful to God, intolerable to itself, and detestable to man.

Personal effort combined with God's limitless divine grace is necessary to acquire humility and root out the vice of pride. This personal effort consists in the calm but forceful opposition to every intimation of vanity or pride by the immediate practice of an act of humility. The constant repetition of such acts results in the acquisition of the moral virtue of humility recommended by St. John in his third admonition against the devil. "Strive ever to humble yourself in word and deed; rejoicing more at another's good than in thine own; desiring that others be preferred to you in all things, and this with all thy heart."[11] This allows for no flattering of self-love in thought, word, or deed while simultaneously it discourages vanity and pride. It unites true charity with humility because we are to rejoice more in our neighbor's welfare than in our own. Yet even this is not sufficient; in addition St. John requires complete self-immolation by preferring our neighbor to ourself in all things. Such a requirement demands great nobility of character because man is called upon to exercise the greatest charity by this total renunciation of self. To place one's neighbor before one's self, at all times, is to practice the highest degree of humility.

All this places a tremendous demand on human nature, yet St. John of the Cross did not consider it to be impossible for religious, whom he presupposed to have a thorough understanding of the virtue of humility and its necessity in religious life. With St. Paul, he could well say, "I speak to them who know the law"[12]— the law of the Gospel and the law of the particular community of which he is a member. These admonitions are directed toward those whose principal profession in life is the glorification of God and their own sanctification, since ". . . those who worship God must do so in spirit and in truth."[13]

If this is not the motive of your religious life, then your life is nothing more than a farce, since without humility nothing is acceptable to God and the proud are an abomination before Him. If genuine humility is not the foundation on which we build, the religious life cannot survive. This is why St. Theresa says, "See how much humility you possess and you can measure your progress toward eternal life."[14]

St. John of the Cross insists that humility is not a mere formality nor disciplinary disposition satisfied with external actions, but a sincere conviction that we are nothing more than what we truly are in the eyes of God. The spirit of sincerity and truth is an ever recurring theme in the teachings of both St. John and St. Theresa. Nothing is to be done through mere routine, nor simply because the work has been assigned to us, but rather with full knowledge that what we do is done with a spirit of sincerity and complete love of God. It is the privilege of such humble souls to overcome evil with an abundance of good. Seawalls form a strong barrier to the waves of the sea and century after century they offer resistance. Eventually, however, they crumble before the steady onslaught. The lowly sand of the shore, on the other hand, offers no opposition to the fury of the same waves but rather calms and destroys their tempestuousness. This is the picture of the proud and the humble. Proud hearts are in continual conflict and mutually injure all they contact. Eventually their pride crumbles and is incorporated into the detestable pride of Satan himself. At the same time the humble meet the same opposition with calmness, abundant goodness is radiated by each success, and they extinguish and destroy the violence of evil.

Nothing is more confusing to the devil than a sincere act of humility, which, as St. John teaches, is more meritorious than the performance of great miracles. Miracles depend upon God for their power; whereas humility freely gives of itself, subjecting all to a Power it recognizes as greater than itself. Each sincere act of humility increases our future glory and is intensely pleasing to God. There is nothing more despicable to the devil than the glory of God and the salvation of souls. Therefore he is completely thwarted in his attempts to seduce souls, who in the moment of such temptations comply with the grace of God and perform acts of humility. The more frequently we humble ourselves before God the more impotent the devil becomes and the soul becomes filled with joy and peace.

This is what St. John meant when he said, "Unless you are truly humble, you will not arrive at perfect charity."[15] Humility is the basis on which we build self-renunciation; and its perfection is total immolation which is absolute charity whereby the soul lives not for itself, but solely for the love and glory of God.

CHAPTER SEVENTEEN

THE SPIRIT OF MORTIFICATION

St. John gives three admonitions to all those who desire to conquer themselves and all sensual desires. "The first is a realization of why one has entered the religious life. It is necessary to realize that religious are human beings and that imperfections and disturbances will arise because of the difference in temperaments and habits. One must train himself to look upon these things as means of obtaining perfection, as they indeed are. The words and actions of others are meant to be the purifying process as well as definite stepping stones along the road to perfection and we must learn to take the best advantage of every such opportunity which presents itself. If we fail to do this we will not overcome our emotions or sensual nature and it will become very difficult to adjust ourselves to the characteristics of those around us. Only by accepting the trials of religious life as a process of purification will we be able to attain freedom from ourselves and peace of heart."[1]

One of man's greatest enemies is himself, because within himself are found many obstacles to virtue, the chief of which is called sensuality, which rises from three interior sources, the mind, the heart, and the flesh. St. John of the Cross terms our own nature "the flesh," because he deems this the most difficult opposition to sanctification. Since much has been written concerning the hardships and conflicts which arise in subduing passion we shall discuss the spirit of these admonitions or the manner of conquering and directing the feelings of repugnance which naturally arise. The first of these considerations will be concerned with the persons with whom we live.

God created man a sociable being, endowing him with understanding and the admirable gift of language so that he might converse with and love his fellow being. Without these gifts man would lead a solitary and unhappy life amidst the joys and beauties of the universe. We learn from Sacred Scripture that God, after He had created all the animals of the earth and the birds of the air, brought them before Adam so he could see them and name them. Yet even though this was an act of royalty and dignity Adam was not completely happy. The vaulted firmament flecked with its myriads of stars; the birds rejoicing in their exquisite plumage and melodious chants; the magnificent garden of Paradise filled with towering trees and beautiful flowers failed to satisfy him completely, because he was alone. All might serve him as king but none was a companion like unto himself, who could reciprocate the love and understanding he longed to share with them. No matter how many material objects may surround man he is lonely without a communion of souls, for each man needs the company of his fellow creatures.

Although God created man a sociable being, we have made this human interchange difficult because of our manifold defects. It is necessary, then, to establish a certain *modus vivendi* called social education, to make human intercourse possible and pleasing. Education, of itself, does not root out individual vices nor does it infallibly produce virtue, rather it places upon the individual the obligation of concealing his own defects lest they annoy others, and of tolerating the weaknesses of others. Those who have the greatest weaknesses and miseries to hide stand in need of the most education. This does not necessarily imply that in the name of virtue the manners and forms of social etiquette invented by man should be neglected. On the contrary, it indicates that one should be fused into the other in order to cultivate mutual good will and esteem. If all men were good and perfect in heart and mind, then there would be no need of formalism because absolute sincerity would magnetize all men and be the only form of social intercourse necessary. Unfortunately, this ideal is not ours, so we must intermingle good social manners while paying attention to our own weaknesses and duly considering another's shortcomings.

Good education is an excellent companion of virtue, for the two are of mutual assistance. Yet we must likewise bear in mind that misuse of the principle of education may cause the danger of concealing what is not really good, but evil. Great virtue combined with an excellent social education should make a person a model of perfect human intercourse.

Christian education requires much more than simple social education since it desires us not only to overlook the defects of our neighbor but to ignore them entirely. Therefore St. Paul says: "Charity thinketh no evil."[2] What cannot be ignored must be tolerated with an open mind for the same Apostle says: "Charity is kind, is patient; charity envieth not, dealeth not perversely; is not puffed up; is not ambitious, seeketh not her own; is not provoked to anger . . . beareth all things, believeth all things, hopeth all things, endureth all things."[3] There is little comparison, then, between a person whose heart is filled with charity combined with social etiquette, and one who simply has been educated socially; because the one who is animated by the nobler sentiments will surely be the more readily accepted and pleasing to his neighbor.

St. John of the Cross wants us not only to bear patiently with the eccentricities of others but he also wants us to profit by them, accepting them as a means of obtaining sanctification. His maxim: ". . . understand well that thou hast come to religious life that all may mold and try thee . . ."[4] shows that we should learn to look upon those with whom we come in contact as the instruments arranged by Divine Providence to deliver us from our pride and egotism. Such an interpretation is incomparably more extensive and beautiful than the idea of mere social education.

The second maxim elucidates the first: "The religious must be firmly convinced that religious life will mold and try him in virtue. The religious is like a rough stone in need of chiseling and polishing before it can be used to advantage, and in this instance the tools of mortification are supplied by those with whom we daily live. For one this is listening cheerfully to what he fain would not hear; for another it is the performance of tasks which he finds completely obnoxious; and for others it is the disciplining of those characteristics which prove troublesome to themselves and their neighbors; while for another it is the repression of the desire to be held in high esteem and affection by his neighbor. Every annoyance is a method of mortification to be endured with inward patience and silence offered for the love of God. Only when a religious allows himself to be thus fashioned can he be made worthy of heaven."[5]

This is a most admirable teaching which provides a wonderful and excellent method of analyzing men and their shortcomings, which are both numerous and varied. Divine Providence permits this multitude of vexations among His faithful servants in order to carry out His divine plan. It is only by understanding and accepting human nature at its best and at its worst that we can realize how what is so repugnant and irritating to some is tolerable and even desirable to others. If the rough stone could only understand, it would cherish the hand of the artist which so pitilessly trims it in order to polish it the more. If this viewpoint of human nature were accepted by all men, soon all sources of dissatisfaction and agitation would disappear, not only in individuals, but in general among all classes of men.

This teaching is not peculiar to the holy doctor of Carmel; it is the natural consequence of the teaching of the Gospel and of the Catholic doctrine of Divine Providence. Even the minutest creature in the universe is of concern to almighty God both conjunctively and individually. For each individual characteristic God has appointed a special end and harmony which co-operate admirably to increase the glory of God and the sanctification of the elect. It was because Christ wished His disciples to understand this doctrine of Divine Providence that He addressed them thus: "Are not two sparrows sold for a farthing? And not one of them shall fall on the ground without your Father [knowing it]. But, the very hairs of your head are all numbered. Fear not, therefore: better are ye than many sparrows."[6] "To them that love God all things work together unto good; and according to His purpose you are all called to be saints."[7] It is evident, then, that for those who have consecrated themselves to God: "This is the will of God, your sanctification."[8]

We know this truth, but deep down in our hearts do we live and abide by its many implications? King David understood well the sanctification which resulted from bearing with his neighbor's deficiencies. When fleeing from his son Absalom he forgave his rebellious subject, Semei, who treated him contumeliously and even resorted to physical violence. To those who asked permission to destroy the insolent servant, David meekly answered: "Let him alone and let him curse; for the Lord hath bid him curse David; and who is he that shall dare say, why hath he done so? Perhaps the Lord may look upon my affliction, and . . . render me good for the cursing of this day."[9] In the reproaches of Semei David saw a dispensation of Divine Providence, permitting him an occasion of practicing heroic virtue.

Thus it is that Divine Providence tries His friends. It is very difficult always to see the image of God in those who are disagreeable to us; nevertheless Providence does foresee and permit all the movements of the human heart as He regulates the thousand varied characteristics of men. Neither the external nor the internal actions of men can be hidden from God. If the very hairs of the children of Adam are numbered, there is more reason to believe that He will not allow to pass unnoticed his many children. God alone can sound the depth of the human heart; and He alone knows the natural antipathy one person may have for another. Nevertheless He permits and even ordains that such people live together, even though they be mutually repulsive to one another, that through their forebearance and mutual love they may attain great moral virtues and high sanctity.

The fact that persons of such different characters and temperaments should live together in the same house and probably discharge the same duties is certainly not a result of mere chance; it is Divine Providence who has disposed or commanded it to be thus. We must train ourselves to believe firmly that those persons who unconsciously or otherwise disturb our peace of mind and reveal to us our lack of self-control are the instruments sent by Divine Providence to help us in our sanctification. An indifference which we take for contempt, and which hurts and irritates us proves how far we really are from the admirable meekness of our Savior. Those words, which may be imprudent but not intentionally so, which seem to us so biting and sarcastic and which so deeply offend our sensitiveness indicates that after many years in religious life there still lurks in our souls much pride and self-love. Perhaps it was for such purposes as these that God places these people near us, to teach us and to show us that which is most difficult to understand, the knowledge of ourselves!

Wounded self-love causes the imagination to distort the offense, making it appear much worse than it really is. This in turn embitters the heart and impels us to treat the offender as we imagine he treats us. It hints with diabolic insistence that the only prudent way to deal with him is to leave him strictly alone, and to regard him with silent contempt. All this reveals how very far we are from the true knowledge of religious life and the means of obtaining sanctity. This is contrary to Christian charity which tells us that we should love our neighbor as we love ourselves. Relative to dealing with this type of person who annoys us St. John gives the excellent advice: "Here indeed we have a great treasure; do not cast it away. Those persons who unconsciously are such a mortification to us, are in reality the means God has chosen for our sanctification. Each day, each hour offer magnificent opportunities to show our love of God who is greatly pleased with our many sacrifices. . . . Wisdom enters through love, silence, and mortification. It is indeed great wisdom to keep silence and not to be annoyed by the words, deeds, or lives of others."[10]

Thus a single act of abnegation and patience performed through pure love has more merit than miracles. It is true that in dealing with persons who annoy us we shall often experience many inconveniences which may tend to embitter us. It is at such times that we are being offered the best opportunities of our lives, if we know how to make good use of them, to humble ourselves, to pray, and to merit. Instead of brooding over uncharitable thoughts, which only act as poison to our minds, we ought to kneel before a crucifix and meditate profoundly on the great humility of the Son of God which merited our redemption. This is a certain means of restoring peace to our minds when they are filled with disturbances. Looked at in the light of the crucifix how small and trivial such things become. Then, if ever, we make perfect acts of humility which really come from the depths of our hearts. What a wealth of knowledge and merit we gain from a few minutes thus spent in quiet recollection. Such a prayer is more efficacious than many months of pious reading and penance. On the final day of reckoning we shall be amazed to see that we are debtors to those who caused us the greatest agitation, far more so than to those who tried to please us and make us happy.

Under no pretense should the sufferings of others be a pleasure to anyone; much less should anyone desire to be the cause of such unhappiness. In ancient Rome where the highest pagan civilization came into contact with the depths of human degradation, distinguished ladies and noble senators experienced a sadistic joy in making human beings suffer. It is incomprehensible how any human being can take pleasure in seeing a fellow human being, or even an animal, suffer. Certainly this was not the doctrine which Christ spread and humbly proclaimed to the entire world from the

Mount of the Beatitudes. Yet even among those who live in the shadow of the cross we find those who take delight in seeing and causing moral suffering. Humanly speaking there is no justifiable explanation for such conduct. There is another group who may fail to recognize themselves as sadists, yet they delight in petty aversion toward their neighbors. This they cloak under the statement, ". . . but I just like to tease him." If the sources of this vain amusement is aversion or pleasure in another's embarrassment, then certainly it is not in conformity with Christian charity. Could such a one who attempts to salve his conscience with the notion that this is but innocent amusement say to God: "O God, I offer Thee the pleasure I have taken today in mortifying my brethren"? Such an act is completely incongruous and bespeaks a perverted moral character.

Despite all this, it is in the design of God that we patiently bear any annoyances which may arise from close living with our fellow religious. In a sense martyrs owe their palm of glory to their executioners. Martyrdom of the spirit is no less pleasing to God than martyrdom of the body — in fact it is a necessary means to sanctification. Yet no matter how beneficial this may be to others certainly no one wants to be consciously guilty of torturing his neighbor, so we should daily pray that God will keep us from being instruments of mortification to others. At the same time, however, we must also ask for the grace to accept graciously and even joyfully any perversity of character with which we might be tried. A person who unconsciously mortifies another gains as much merit as the one who, with great heroism accepts the mortification.

This explains the exceptional, and for the world incomprehensible, psychology of the saints, with their repugnance to praise and flattery and their sincere gratitude for those who mortified them most. No cause for wonder, then, when we read in the *Interior Castle* of St. Theresa: "Souls who have learned to suffer persecution have a great interior joy and possess much peace of soul. They bear no enmity toward those who ill treat them, nor do they desire to do so. Indeed they conceive a special love for their persecutors, so that, if they see them in trouble, they are deeply grieved and would do anything possible to relieve them. They lovingly recommend them to God in prayer and rejoice if some of the favors God has destined for them He gives to their enemies instead. Everything they do is for the purpose of preventing any offense from being offered to God."[11]

This is the concept of religious life as St. John would have us live it. "If anyone does not wish to accept and seek for mortification in religious life, he should have remained in the world, seeking his own comfort, honor, and praise."[12] Religious life viewed in such a manner causes daily life with its insignificant details to become a treasury of great merits. What seemed intolerable defects in others can be converted into excellent opportunities to practice heroic acts of virtue. "One benefits by every incident."[13] Inspired by martyrs such as St. Ignatius, who provoked the wild beasts to destroy his body so that his precious soul would soon enjoy celestial happiness, and Christian virgins who cherished the hand of the executioner, let us learn to suffer with patience and joy the unsympathetic characteristics of those with whom we have to live, remembering they afford us many occasions of acquiring great merits.

The person who perseveres in daily mortification will have no less merit before God than the martyr who offers his neck to the executioner. All those who are consecrated to God by religious profession must aspire to such a prolonged martyrdom of mind and heart; and it is often those who are aiming at the same goal as ourselves who will cause us the most mortification. This is the genuine spirit of St. John of the Cross. If any one doubts it, let him read and assiduously meditate on the admonition of the saint: ". . . if thou fail to observe these things, you will not be able to overcome your sensual nature or your emotions; neither will you be able to conduct yourself agreeably with other religious; finally unless you train yourself to cheerful acceptance of daily mortification you will not attain to everlasting happiness and peace."[14]

CHAPTER EIGHTEEN

SELF-ABNEGATION

The second admonition of St. John regarding the conquest of self is: "Never fail to perform any works which in themselves may be repugnant to you if they have been commanded in obedience. Do not fulfill such duties simply because they are pleasing to you; on the contrary, it behooves you to perform all actions with equanimity otherwise it is impossible to gain constancy and overcome sensuality."[1]

The principal element in every human action from which it derives its merit or its guilt is the end and intention for which man performs a deliberate act. Intentions can be reduced to two, pleasure and duty, since the reason why we do anything is either to obtain pleasure from so doing or because we must fulfill some obligation of conscience. The nobler of the two is duty.

God created all things and being infinitely wise He attached pleasure to both spiritual and physical actions, so that man would be stimulated to fulfill his duty. According to God's intention pleasure is meant to be a stimulus, or a means, to duty, not the end. Therefore one who performs his actions for the sake of pleasure only, sooner or later acts in a manner which is detrimental to nature. The brute beast has no other motive nor stimulus in its actions than instinct and pleasure. For man to follow such a course is to weaken his will and reduce him to the level of a slave to his own passions. This is well exemplified in the history of Solomon. He besought the Lord with much insistence and humility not to give him what his eyes coveted or his heart desired.[2] Yet, he who erected and dedicated the most magnificent temple in the world to the God of Israel, fell into the most repugnant vices, despite his great prudence and incomparable wisdom, and erected temples to the idols of Chamos and Moloch and adored them.[3]

One of the greatest scourges that God can send to men and to nations is to permit them to idolize pleasure. It was thus He punished the infidelity of the ancient people: Wherefore God gave them up to the desires of their hearts.[4] In like manner God chastised His chosen people: "My people heard not My voice; and Israel harkened not to me. So I let them go according to the desires of their heart; they shall walk in their own inventions."[5]

Such instances show the need of man's regulating his desires for all that is pleasing to his senses. In his admonition, St. John tells us that we should not be swayed by our natural inclination for pleasure and omit any action, no matter how disagreeable it may be, provided it is for the greater glory of God. To act merely from pleasure is irrational and places man on the level of the beasts. The Holy Ghost warns us to control our passions carefully because "men blaspheme whatever things they know not; as well as that which they naturally know. In these actions they become corrupted like irrational creatures." St. Paul teaches the same doctrine: "The sensual man perceiveth not these things that are of the spirit of God; for it is foolishness to him."[6] Thus do they degenerate little by little who follow the path of pleasure.

St. John's teachings on how to regulate our natural inclination for pleasure are marvelously expounded not only in his admonitions but in the *Ascent of Mount Carmel*. He terms pleasure as the affections of the senses whereby man uses his heart, mind, memory, or will in order to derive pleasure. The misuse of these faculties lead to manifold disorders while perfect control accrues great virtue. His knowledge of the human soul portrayed in the *Ascent* has rightly placed him as one of the foremost psychologists of the world. There is no nook or corner of the mind or heart of man which escapes the eye of this keen observer; nowhere else can we find so profound yet so clear an explanation of the relations which exist between God and man. The entire work is prolific with quotations from the Bible and seems to be not the work of man but that of one inspired by God Himself.

St. John tells us that we must place all our affections in God alone. "He that loves a creature is only as great as the one he loves; for love not only makes the lover equal to the object of his love but in some instances even subjects him to it. It follows, then, that the soul who loves anyone less than God is incapable of pure union with God and transformation into Him."[7] To take pleasure in creatures for their own sake is to lose our liberty: "The soul that longs for freedom of desire is treated and considered in the eyes of God, not as a son, but as a base slave and captive. . . . Therefore such a soul can never attain the true liberty of spirit which is encompassed in Divine Union. For slavery can have no part in liberty, and liberty cannot dwell in a heart that is subjected to its own desires, for such is the heart of a slave; rather true freedom is to be found in the heart which places its entire pleasure in God."[8]

While disorderly affections rule the heart of man he will never know complete satisfaction. All creatures will be but crumbs which have fallen from the table of God. Wherefore, he who feeds only upon these crumbs is ever hungering, and rightly so, because crumbs serve only to whet the appetite, not to appease it. As the prophet Isaias says, "the heart of one filled with earthly desires is as a tempestuous sea . . . there is no peace for the wicked, saith the Lord God."[9]

In this same chapter of the *Ascent* St. John explains the five effects produced by pleasure in the soul: "Pleasure wearies, torments, darkens, defiles, and weakens the soul. . . . The ever demanding desires of the soul make it restless and discontented, bringing great weariness and fatigue to the soul. Even though such a one were to obtain its greatest desires, still it would not be satisfied; for broken cisterns cannot contain the water necessary to slake a burning thirst."[10] Thus Isaias says, "Man is faint with thirst, and his soul is empty."[11] Again the soul filled with many desires is as a man burning with fever; nothing satisfies his thirst until the fever leaves him. We read in the book of Job: "When he shall be filled he shall be straitened; he shall burn, and every sorrow shall fall upon him. . . . The heavens shall reveal his iniquity, and the earth shall rise up against him."[12]

Thus the soul which is ever attempting to fulfill its own desires knows no real happiness or content. To this purpose Jeremias said, "In the desire of his heart he extinguished the fire of his love."[13] Even as a lover is wearied and fatigued on the day of his greatest hopes, so overindulgence in natural desires leaves in its wake nothing but emptiness and hunger; for desire is like a raging fire which only increases when more fuel is added. How true it is that none of having this desire is fully satisfied. It may well be that when fuel is consumed by the fire the flame decreases; yet in human desires this is not true; the more fuel consumed the more the soul thirsts and hungers; for indulgence only increases longing.[14]

What in the beginning may have seemed only a slight and innocent passion will, if neglected and fostered, soon cause the ravages in the soul that St. John has so clearly defined and will serve as a great impediment on the road to perfection. For the saint continues: "Those who burden themselves with extraordinary penances are ignorant of the true meaning of mortification. They may think that they are performing sufficient penance to unite themselves to Divine Wisdom but their error is lamentable. If they labored more diligently to curb their desires they would achieve a greater degree of union than possible by mere external mortifications. Unless the earth is tilled it will bear nothing but weeds, in like manner mortification of desires is necessary for the growth of the soul. However many efforts we may make, without this mortification the soul will make no progress in the knowledge of God or itself and will achieve little or no perfection.[15]

No man can rely on the gifts which he thinks he possesses and fully indulge his affection or desires without becoming blinded to his own folly and degraded in the eyes of God. Who would have thought a man as prudent and filled with wisdom as Solomon would in his old age adore false idols? The only way to avoid such evils is to train ourselves to overlook the pleasure or displeasure we may find in the execution of our daily works. Desires have no place in the actions of persons who have consecrated themselves to God. A superior once questioned a religious concerning the choice of a new assignment and the answer given was: "I beg your Reverence not to ask me what I prefer, but rather tell me what I have to do." There is an answer worthy of a true religious!

To perform actions from the motive of duty requires great virtue and strength of character, especially when there is no external fame or honor attached to such actions. It is true that in the course of life we meet with more actions which are repugnant to us than those which are filled with honor and to fulfill these assignments, because it is our duty to do so, requires such heroic efforts against the strongest inclinations of nature that only great and noble characters will be able to maintain peace and happiness throughout the conflict. To be constantly going against our desires is no mere trifle, yet no one has become perfect in the midst of the clamor and pursuit of worldly affairs because noble hearts are trained only in the field of humility and self-abnegation.

For eighteen years the Son of God lived a life of solitude and obscurity in Nazareth, where he labored in the humble workshop of a poor carpenter. The secret of imitating Jesus and Mary lies in the fulfillment of duty from a sense of humility and self-abnegation, which increases will power and brings the soul closer to God. Those who seek self and vain glory in their actions by avoiding as much as possible what is disagreeable to their senses behave like children, for they have not yet attained to the full use of reason. Their actions are not in accord with the dictates of their conscience and, motivated as they are by self-love, they foster such evils as pride, selfishness, and hardheartedness toward one's fellowman. The self-seekers never know complete satisfaction in their works, for what appears agreeable now suddenly becomes distasteful, and what seems honorable today, will be dishonorable and disgraceful tomorrow. Thus, the self-seeker knows no stability because his character is as changeable as his selfishness and inconstancy.

Pleasure is a bad counselor on which to rely. Because of this St. John warns us: "Do not expect your guardian angel to motivate your desires but rather to illuminate your reason, since reason and understanding are sufficient for the performance of a virtuous deed."[16] The sensual appetites are never satisfied. The more they are catered to, the more they mortify and torment us. "If you fulfill your desires, you will reap a double measure of bitterness; therefore learn to limit your desires even though you obtain no pleasure from so doing."[17]

He who seeks his own gratification loses all merit in the eyes of God. When he finally stands at the judgment seat of God, He will say to him: "Thou hast already received thy reward. Thy lips may have proclaimed that thy works were done for Me but in your heart this was not so. Your works of charity may have seemed laudable to the world but they were nothing more than gratification of your self-love. You have, at times, spoken well of Me, but here again you were but seeking your own glory, not Mine. Even your devotions and religious actions have been more for the purpose of satisfying your sensible pleasures than of doing My will."

Not only, then, do we lose the merit of our good works by

self-gratification, but they bring down terrible chastisement from God. "We must believe that when we vainly rejoice over some pleasure, God is preparing some bitter punishment, so that the pain which results from these illicit pleasures will greatly surpass the joy."[18] To forego the misery of losing all merits, the primary motive of all our actions must be to please God. "The spiritual man must not rejoice in temporal things. He must fear lest once he yields to his desires they will but grow in intensity. . . . He must learn to restrain the first motion of his heart toward creatures, remembering the truth that man should strive to increase the honor and glory of God in all things."[19]

We find a beautiful example of this in the Gospel. Our Lord sent the seventy-two disciples to preach throughout the cities, saying: "Go, behold I send you as lambs among wolves."[20] Having fulfilled His command they returned to Him completely satisfied with the first fruits of their mission: "Lord, the devils are also subject to us in Thy Name." But the Lord, wishing to regulate and increase their spiritual joy, gently said, "Behold I have given you power to tread upon serpents and scorpions, . . . and nothing shall hurt you. Yet rejoice not . . . that spirits are subject unto you; but rejoice . . . that your names are written in heaven."[21] Our Lord did not wish the disciples to be self-complacent even over their miracles; rather He wished them to remember that all their works were done for the glory of God and the salvation of souls.

The faithful observance of this doctrine teaches us to control our natural inclinations fully, so that even trivial actions will give more glory to God and we shall enjoy great peace of soul. Yet even in this knowledge we must not take too much satisfaction because St. John warns us, "The most delicate flower withers quickly and soon loses its fragrance. Therefore beware of seeking spiritual delights for this will lead to inconstancy. Choose rather a spiritual vigor which will properly regulate all creature affections. Then you will find peace and sweetness in abundance."[22]

The purpose of depriving our sensual nature is not to weaken our faculties but rather to raise them to the supernatural level where they belong. To harbor the thought that deprivation is degradation is most derogatory to St. John of the Cross as well as to any other master of religious perfection, since it is attributing to them the intent of mutilating human nature. Nothing could be more destructive to religious fervor than to harbor such untrue thoughts. Neither was mutilation the purpose nor the correct interpretation of St. John's doctrine. Rather would he show us that the only road which can lead to complete union with God is that filled with deprivations of material objects which are but obstacles on the road to perfection.

Just as the farmer mercilessly prunes the trees and leaves them in an apparently pitiable condition that they may produce more abundant flowers and fruit, so, too, must we interpret the doctrine of self-love which this great master of the human spirit apparently completely destroys. The main purpose of his writings is to teach us how to deprive our faculties and senses of what apparently seems so necessary to them. Unless the reader understands the saint's teaching on this point, he will become discouraged in his search for perfection. The saint does not wish to stifle any legitimate faculty, but rather to cleanse it from the thousand imperfections contracted from the world, so that once purified it may, with the assistance of divine grace, begin to manifest all the moral and intellectual beauties of which God has made man capable. The teachings of mortification, relative to self-abnegation, are found in these words of St. John of the Cross: "Self denial in sensual pleasure brings tremendous spiritual benefits. That which was irrational becomes rational; that which was earthly becomes celestial. The man who seeks material pleasures, rejoicing in his accomplishments, merits no other title than sensual and temporal; while he who rejoices in the supernatural may be called spiritual and eternal."[23]

The third benefit to be derived from practicing the saint's doctrine of self-abnegation is that once the will has strengthened itself to accept duty without pleasure, its happiness is greatly increased. Did not Christ Himself say: "They shall receive a hundredfold"[24] in this life. It follows, then, that simple pleasures foregone in this life are rewarded both temporally and spiritually a hundredfold. Once the eye is purged of sensual joys a spiritual joy comes to the soul which enables it to see God reflected in every material object which it perceives. The same is true of the purification of all other senses. Even as the state of innocence increased the joy of our first parents, so when the sensual part of our nature is subjected to reason there follows a delightful knowledge and contemplation of

God. "Wherefore to him that is pure, all things, whether high or low, are an occasion of greater good and further purity. The man who is directed by sensual pleasure alone cannot enjoy the habitual presence of God. . . . Hence it follows that being pure in heart, a man finds in all things a knowledge of God which is joyful and pleasant, pure and spiritual, serene and loving."[25]

Although no one was more austere than St. John in his practices, yet no one could equal him in his sweetness of spirit and gentleness of character. His life was a practical demonstration of the admirable teaching of self-abnegation yet the intimate happiness he shared with God was evident in all his words and works. With the Apostle, St. Paul, he could say, "With Christ I am nailed to the cross". . .[26] but in the midst of my tribulations I am filled with consolation and supreme joy: "For to me, to live is Christ; and to die is gain."[27]

CHAPTER NINETEEN

THE BASIC VIRTUES

The great ascetic is not satisfied with simply denying ourselves pleasure in the execution of our works. He further recommends that "the spiritual man shall never look for what is most pleasurable to him because this leads to attachment. Neither must he turn from what is displeasing to him, but rather seek what is toilsome and distasteful. In this way he bridles his sensual nature fully. To do otherwise is to increase love of self and to lose the love of God."[1]

Thus we deliberately choose what is difficult and painful to what is delightful and easy, not only accepting these things with resignation but cherishing and appreciating them as something indispensable to our perfection. Such is the remarkable teaching of the most tender lover of the cross. The following counsel is given to the soul about to ascend the first steps of the mystical mountain of perfection: "Whatever pleasure that presents itself to the sense which is not purely for God's honor and glory must be completely renounced for love of God." While here on earth Christ never sought for pleasure; He simply desired to do His Father's will in all things. This renunciation of the senses is to be treated in the following manner: "If some great pleasure presents itself to our sense of hearing, then we must not desire to listen to it. Do not give in to the pleasures of sight, unless such objects bring you closer to God. This same ruling should apply to the sense of speech and all the senses wherein a pleasure presents itself as a distraction from pure contemplation on the things of God."[2] Because St. John of the Cross desires to regulate the corporal sense and the affections of the soul he gives the following maxims:

> "Strive always to choose not that which is easiest but that which is most difficult;
> Not that which is most delectable, but that which is most displeasing;
> Not that which gives most pleasure, but that which gives the least;

122

Not that which is most restful, but that which is wearisome:
Not that which gives consolation, but rather that which is depressing;
Not that which is greatest, but that which is least;
Not that which is loftiest and most precious, but that which is lowest
and most despised;
Not that which is a desire for anything, but that which is a desire
for nothing.
To go about seeking not the best things but the worst.
Strive to desire to enter into complete detachment and poverty with
respect to all worldly objects solely for the love of God."

"It is advisable to subject your will completely to the wishes of
God, accepting these maxims with all your heart. Once you can
accomplish this then your soul will be filled with peace and contentment, and you will act with order and discretion."[3]

According to this doctrine which is the synthesis of St. John's
asceticism, we should always prefer the difficult to that which is
easy, the unpleasant and laborious to that which is pleasant and
consoling; that which humbles and depresses us to all that can
honor and exalt us. Whenever the choice is left to us we should
choose that which is most humble and difficult to do and leave to
others that which is most pleasing and honorable. This doctrine
also contains a recommendation for cheerful acceptance of suffering in whatever form it may come to us be it physical or moral,
corporal or spiritual. This is not spineless conformity to the ways
and conventions of the world, but rather it presupposes a high
degree of self-renunciation and complete abandonment to the will
of God at all times. Sufferings will inevitably accompany a perfect
performance of duty and demands patience and fortitude. This
takes a truly great character who will not withdraw from duty
when confronted with obstacles and hardships, and the acid test
is the performance of the most ordinary tasks of life both promptly
and cheerfully. To face continued suffering with peace of mind
and cheerfulness of heart reveals a superior soul, since suffering
ordinarily renders people remiss in their duties.

Yet even this acceptance of sufferings is not enough for St. John.
He desires us to entertain a preference for suffering; he wishes us
to seek after it as we would seek a most cherished object. Such a
demand seems contrary to nature itself. Pain is always a want of
something apprehended as good, or as St. Thomas Aquinas says:
"Pain is an evil to the sufferer."[4]

It may seem paradoxical to say that suffering, in itself, is evil for the one enduring it, and yet it is the source of tremendous blessings. From experience we know the truth of this statement. No matter how bitter a medicine may be, a patient will take it if he knows it will restore his health. So, too, with suffering. No saint ever declared that a physical or moral suffering in itself was a desirable good. The saints loved suffering and recommended it because of the benefits coming from it, which may be reduced to these four groups: First, suffering expiates and satisfies for a wrongdoing. Every satisfaction of sensual pleasures contracts a debt due to justice. The more intense the disorderly pleasure, the greater the debt, as we read in the Apocalypse: "As much as she hath glorified herself, and lived in delicacies, so much torment and sorrow give ye to her."[5] This is applicable not only to great disorders but also to the many insignificant faults which are so easily committed in our daily life. Very often we fail because of the desire for some trifling pleasure or to avoid certain hardships. For each minute disorder we contract a proportionate debt of suffering or pain, for our divine Redeemer tells us "that every idle word that men shall speak they shall render an account for it on the day of judgment. For by thy words thou shalt be justified and by thy words thou shalt be condemned."[6]

The life of every man, however orderly it may seem, is full of such discrepancies. Therefore David has said well: "Evils without number have surrounded me; my iniquities have overtaken me, and I was not able to see."[7] Nothing shall go unpunished by divine Justice: "Every one of us shall render an account to God for himself."[8] and ". . . fire shall try every man's work."[9] For every disorderly affection, however slight, we must pass through the fire of patient love here on this earth or through the consuming fire of the next world. If man does not purify himself in this life by voluntary penance, accepting and supporting with resignation a suffering proportionate to his disorderly pleasures, a terrible justice will purify him afterward. We read in the Old Testament: "If we do not penance, we shall fall into the hands of the Lord."[10] It is incomparably easier to purify ourselves here rather than hereafter, because here, sufferings are voluntary and free, and God in His infinite mercy is moved to overlook the sins of men when they are sincerely penitent. Our Lord said to this effect: "While thou art in the way [to the prince with thine adversary], endeavor to be delivered from him; lest perhaps he draw thee to the judge; and the judge deliver thee to the exacter, and the exacter cast thee into prison. I say to thee, thou shalt not go out from thence until thou pay the very last farthing."[11]

While it is true that Christ satisfied for our sins and the sins of the entire world, the words of St. Paul to the Colossians are also true: "I . . . rejoice in my sufferings for you, and fill up those things that are wanting in the sufferings of Christ in my flesh."[12]

It is evident that nothing is wanting to the sufferings of Christ which may be applied to us, except our co-operation. Sufferings also contain a great expiatory power. For this reason, those who are truly sorry for their sins and desire to appease the divine Justice carefully seek and lovingly embrace all manner of suffering. This was the doctrine of the greatest as well as the least among the saints.

The second great effect of suffering is purification. Pleasures more or less sinful, not only render the soul a debtor to divine Justice but they also weaken it. Every member of the human nature still bears within him the effects of the first disorderly affection of Adam and this inherent weakness increases with each personal sin committed. Suppose a person to be in possession of youth and beauty; the proud possessor of many talents and charms, while goodness and faith are added to his potentialities. If such a person never knows suffering of any kind, he will soon begin to deteriorate. The reason for this is that the more he possesses the more he desires, the more he desires the greater is his incapability of complete fulfillment, for which of us having that which he most desired is completely satisfied? In time it will be noticed that, paradoxical as it seems, such a one will reach the state where he will repel even while he charms, because continued pleasure, not tempered with suffering, creates and fosters a despicable pride and selfishness.

Now consider one who has been tried by suffering. He uses these crosses to the best advantages and thus intensifies his patience and love, while he becomes ever more understanding of human nature around him. This soul, deprived of many pleasures, has been given many gifts, because it knows well the message of suffering. It has been freed from selfishness; it loves with a deeper purity and constancy, and it knows complete freedom of spirit, resembling in some degree the blessed in heaven. It must be remembered though that no soul reaches such heights without first having suffered and wept much. Suffering and love are the two wings that elevate the soul in this life; while suffering without love embitters and degrades. Suffering, sustained by love, is necessary to purify souls in this world, otherwise the purification will take place hereafter. Therefore St. John of the Cross recommends that chosen souls suffer their purgatory in this world through the dark night of loving fire.

The chief object of purgatory is the purification of souls from the stains contracted by sin. Once these effects have been removed the fire of purgatory can no longer affect the soul, even in the midst of flames: "For the fire would have no power over them if they were ready for union with God and had paid for their imperfections, which are the material on which the fire of Purgatory feeds. Once that material is consumed there is nothing left that can burn. One may be certain that the cheerful acceptance of sufferings will obliterate imperfections, suffering of soul will cease, and joy and peace of soul will result."[13]

Consequently, the valiant soul that suffers its purification in this world, shortens or completely eliminates its purgatory in this world and reaches such a state that the fires of purgatory can have no power over it. "As spirits are purged in the next life with dark material fire, so in this life they are purified and enlightened with the dark spiritual fire of love. The difference is that in the next life they are purified with fire, while here below they are cleansed and illumined by love."[14] Since the saints had such an exalted idea of suffering, it is not strange that they accepted suffering willingly and joyfully.

The third power of suffering is impetratory. Nothing in the moral order is more powerful than sincere tears, which are the language of the soul that loves and suffers. Those who suffer without love do not weep, but ordinarily blaspheme. The language of sincere tears is such that it can be resisted by comparatively few because God has so willed it that the heart should naturally yield before patient and loving suffering. Tears can obtain what a smile cannot.

It is the same with God. He reveals His love and beneficence through the goodness which we find in the human heart. He declares that when the sufferer approaches Him He can deny him nothing. "Because . . . thy heart was softened . . . and wept before Me, I also have heard thee."[15] Solomon says: "Though in the sight of men they suffered torments; their hope is full of immortality."[16] Joyfully St. Paul exclaims: "I know Him in whom I believed, therefore I am not ashamed to suffer."[17] Such acceptance of suffering was praised by Christ who proclaimed blessed those who mourned, those who hungered and thirsted after justice; in short, all those who suffered. He promised splendid rewards for each suffering borne with resignation, as well as special blessings to those who were merciful to the sufferer: "Deliver him that suffereth wrong out of the hand of the proud: . . . and thou shalt be as the obedient son of the most High, and He will have mercy on thee more than a mother."[18]

The majority of miracles wrought by Christ were the result of His compassion for sufferers. Notice the afflicted and desolate widow who accompanied her only son to the grave; the tender and affectionate father who wept over his dead daughter; and the bereaved sisters who mourned inconsolably over their dead brother. How compassionate and loving Christ was toward them! The tender heart of Christ was so moved at the sufferings of these people that He performed three of His greatest miracles by restoring their loved ones to life. "The mountains shall be moved and the hills shall tremble; but my mercy shall not depart from thee, . . . O poor little one, tossed with tempest, without all comfort."[19] Truly nothing is so efficacious with God as suffering borne with faith and love.

Suffering renders us Christlike. According to St. Paul, God admits to His glory those who are made conformable to the image of His Son.[20] And there is no other way for this likeness to be accomplished than by suffering, as Christ Himself has said: "If any man will come after Me, let him deny himself, and take up his cross, and follow Me."[21] "He that taketh not up His cross, nor followeth Me, is not worthy of Me."[22] Little wonder, then, that the saints considered it a special grace to be able to suffer something for Christ; for as St. Paul said to the Philippians: "Unto you it is given for Christ, not only to believe in him, but also to suffer for him."[23]

For men of great faith this life is of value only in so far as they can suffer for God. This same thought is beautifully expressed by St. John of the Cross: "Desire to resemble Christ in suffering, to be humiliated and crucified if need be, for if your life is not thus an imitation of His, it is worth nothing. . . . What does he know who does not know how to suffer? The greater and deeper the sufferings, the nearer a soul draws to the crucified Christ."[24] No man will ever be able to fathom the infinite love of our Lord hanging on a cross to redeem the world by the deepest of sufferings. Ever since the cross has been the symbol of love and suffering and an irresistible attraction for the saints, St. Paul wept to think that there could be enemies of the cross of Christ: "God forbid that I should glory; save in the cross of our Lord Jesus Christ; by whom the world is crucified to me, and I to the world."[25] St. John of the Cross did not know how to live without the cross: "It is expedient that like our Beloved, we glory in His cross. Sufferings purify and strip us of the dearest treasures of our hearts so that the greatest sacrifices will conceive a greater love."[26]

The cross is the pilgrim's staff, which is necessary for ease and comfort on the road of life; it is the arms which we use to conquer our enemies; it is the tree of life under which Jesus espoused human nature and now espouses the souls that love Him.

In confirmation of all this let us recall the beautiful instruction given by Christ Himself to His favored daughter, St. Theresa: "Do you think, daughter, that merit consists in fruition? Merit consists in working, suffering and loving. Thou hast never heard of St. Paul that he enjoyed heavenly visions but once, yet innumerable were his sufferings. My entire life was filled with sufferings, but once on Mt. Tabor, was I filled with glory. Do you think that when My Mother held Me in her arms that she experienced joy exclusive of suffering? From the moment of the prophecy of Simeon she was enlightened, not only knowing My sufferings but sharing them with Me. The great saints, led by the Holy Spirit into the desert, performed heavy penances and waged great battles between the devil and themselves; yet they, too, knew long periods without any spiritual consolation. Believe Me, daughter, it is to those most loved by My Father, that He sends His greatest trials, for suffering and love are inseparable. How can I better show thee My love than by willing for thee what I have willed for Myself? Behold My wounds; no pain, you will ever know, will equal these. Thy sufferings help Me to weep for the perdition which materialistic souls are reaping for themselves. Here in patience and joyful acceptance of suffering wilt thou find thy reward."[27] After such a revelation need one wonder that St. Theresa chose for her motto: "To suffer or to die"?

The vehement desires of the saints for suffering arose from a fear of the justice of God, to be administered, not so much to themselves as to others. They deplored most bitterly the deformity caused in the soul by sin, while they realized fully the tremendous power of suffering for the purification of souls. Likewise they realized that man's greatest glory consists in the perfect imitation of Christ, the Man of Sorrows, acquainted with every infirmity,[28] which resemblance cannot be accomplished in heaven if it is not first begun and continued here on earth. Thus the saints esteemed wise, honorable, and joyful what men considered folly, disgrace, and ignominy. Such an interpretation easily explains the logic and harmony of the thoughts, words, and deeds of the saints and men of great faith. It likewise explains the thoughts and actions of the materialistic minded who regard suffering as a misfortune and something to be avoided at any cost.

We who have the honor of having consecrated ourselves to God, and who have so many times knelt at the feet of the Savior, cannot plead ignorance of the great mystery of suffering nor of the wonderful graces God has concealed under suffering; neither can we refuse to accept what is so repugnant to our poor human nature. We took the resolution to bear all sufferings patiently when we embraced the religious state; to refuse to do so would be cowardice as well as an insult to the divine Savior, who first trod the road of suffering, for did not Christ say to us: "No man putting his hand to the plough, and looking back, is fit for the kingdom of God."[29] "The kingdom of heaven suffereth violence, and the violent bear it away."[30] The road which leads to eternal bliss is narrow and rugged; if we do not wish to slip through fatigue or discouragement, it is necessary to lean on the staff of mortification and suffering.

Now we understand clearly why St. John of the Cross says it is not enough to bear patiently what is bitter and distasteful, but we must *seek* and *embrace* that which is difficult and painful; otherwise we cannot conquer self-love or sensuality. The sufferings and hardships we may experience can be reduced to three classes: the first is imposed by our state of life; the second, are the results of the personal circumstances in which each individual finds himself; and the third, are those which result from our free choice.

All the hardships entailed in the performance of duties subject to the rule and the superiors comprise the first class of sufferings. Before binding himself by vow, one should meditate frequently on these obligations, fasts, penances, abnegation of will and judgment, a thousand privations, long hours of prayer, withdrawal from worldly affairs, all these are a part of the religious life. Any attempts to dispense oneself from the observance of any of these things shows a misunderstanding of the sacrifices which are inherent to religious profession. Dispensations can be given by lawful authority but if such dispensations are sought at the outset of religious life, what is the purpose of binding oneself to the religious life at all? If one is tempted to abandon his duty rather than to suffer any inconvenience, then he would do well to ponder on the words of St. Paul to the Galatians: "Are you so foolish, that whereas you began in the spirit, you would now be made perfect by the flesh?"[31]

The first degree of mortification, then, consists in the acceptance of all vexations or hardships which directly result from the rule and its observance. Anyone who proves habitually negligent in fulfilling the rule and tries, for various reasons, to escape his obligations, has not climbed even one step of the high mountain of religious perfection. To him may aptly be applied the words of St. John of the Cross: "If you did not enter religion to carefully fulfill the obligations of your profession, you had no cause to do so, but should have remained in the world, seeking your own comfort, honor, credit and ease."[32]

To the second class of sufferings belong all those hardships not directly dependent on the rule but rather on the circumstances in which we are placed, such as sickness, incompatible companions, or places of abode. Without failing to comply with the letter of the rule we may legitimately seek dispensation from some of these annoyances, such as asking for a transfer to another house, or seeking to change an occupation for which we are unsuited. Yet the soul which trains itself to resignation and acceptance of any hardship that presents itself, mortifies its own selfishness and, if it perseveres, will soon reach the height of perfection.

The third degree of suffering has been reached by those relatively few persons who have lost their fear of suffering, but rather knowing and understanding its inestimable value, love it and seek it. This is especially true regarding sufferings of a spiritual nature which are directed against pride and selfishness. This is the most excellent state and is highly recommended by St. John; to seek all that is most irksome to human nature, especially in spiritual matters, since sufferings which kill self-love borne with patience and resignation advance a person greatly on the road to perfection. To persons in this state are addressed the following words: "What wealth the soul possesses that perfectly understands that it cannot attain to the wisdom and riches of God without entering into the deepest of sufferings, even to the point of seeking therein its consolations and desires. The soul that desires divine Wisdom must first desire suffering, for the only gate whereby one may enter into such riches is the Cross, which is both narrow and filled with suffering. The desire to enter therein belongs to few, but the desire for the joys which result, belongs to many."[33]

Commenting on the passage in which our Lord says: "If any man will follow Me, let him deny himself, and take up his cross, and follow Me. For whosoever will save his life, shall lose it; and whosoever shall lose his life for My sake . . . shall save it,"[34] St. John writes: "Would that we could understand, practice, and experience this counsel of self-denial recommended by our Savior! How differently then would spiritual persons conduct themselves! How many there are who think perfection can be attained by a reformation of life, or by continued prayer and mortification, yet who never seek detachment or denial in their interior life. . . . When perfect spirituality presents itself in the form of annihilation of all sweetness, in aridity and trial, they flee from it as if it were death. Herein they become enemies of the Cross of Christ; for true spirituality seeks, for God's sake, that which is distasteful to what is delectable; inclines itself to suffering rather than to consolation; desires to go without all blessings rather than to possess them . . . and all this from a pure love of God."[35]

If after frequent and assiduous meditation on suffering, as explained by St. John, we still find ourselves lacking the virtues necessary to attain such heights, let us pray for the grace to accept with resignation any suffering which is unavoidable in daily religious life.

CHAPTER TWENTY

SPIRIT OF CARMEL

Although St. John of the Cross was not the founder of a religious order, he was, under the inspiration and guidance of the great St. Theresa of Jesus, one of the principal factors in the reformation of the very ancient order of Carmel of which he was already a professed member. Having been formed according to the spirit of the prophetic observance he was perfectly adapted to revive in all its pristine splendor the ancient spirit of the order of the Blessed Virgin. Consequently it is sufficient to follow him from the moment he met St. Theresa until the time of his death to be convinced that the predominant idea to which he consecrated all his energies was to found new convents, regenerating the ancient fervor of Carmel. This he did by his writings and instructions, as well as by the spiritual direction which he personally gave to its members.

His work, the *Ascent of Mount Carmel,* is more or less general in character and can be read with profit by all who desire to attain religious perfection, although actually they may never reach any degree of supernatural contemplation. The preface of this book is dedicated to these privileged souls: "It is not my principal intent to address all, but rather chosen friars and nuns of the sacred Order of Mt. Carmel, whom God has chosen for greater perfection, because they are already detached from the things of the world, and thus will better understand these instructions concerning detachment of the spirit."[1]

The fundamental doctrine applicable to all who wish to live the spirit of Carmel is to be found in his celebrated *Counsels.* These general principles are necessary for every religious animated by good will and desirous of attaining evangelical perfection. Therefore the preface of this book is dedicated to all religious: "Whoever habitually performs the labors enjoined on him to the best of his ability will progress rapidly to great perfection, gaining many virtues

132

and attaining holy peace."[2] These Counsels are to be considered as real precepts of virtue necessarily practiced by all who desire religious perfection. "If you do not observe these counsels you have not yet learned to be a religious. There is no other way of freeing yourself from imperfections resulting from creature attachments. Many religious, forgetting this truth, have been ruined in their pursuit of perfection by the devil."[3]

The holy prophet Elias first outlined the distinctive characteristics of the true religious spirit and is venerated and recognized by the ancient order of Carmel as its founder and Father. His doctrine is paradoxical; great austerity and ineffable sweetness; continuous retirement and prodigious enterprise. From the vast solitude of the desert he contemplated in symbolic form the grandeur of the Immaculate Mother, venerating and leading others to a veneration of the Mother of chaste love and sweet hope. In the food and drink served him by the angel under the juniper tree, he contemplated the perfect type of the Sacrament of Love. Notwithstanding his ardent affection for solitude and communion with God, he left his retirement when compelled to do so by necessity, to chastise the blasphemer, to rebuke kings and tyrants, and to remind people of the fulfillment of their duties. The powers given him by God were tremendous. He called down fire from heaven when it was necessary for him to prove his mission. He commanded a drought as a punishment over Israel for three years and six months; later, at his command, fertilizing rains replenished the land.[4] His doctrine plus the teachings of Christ, the First Principle and perfect Model of the religious life, form the fundamental spirit of the Order of Carmel. Later this same spirit was revived in all its vigor and perfection by St. Theresa of Jesus and St. John of the Cross. While the elements of the teachings of St. Theresa and St. John may not appear to have the same harmony and intensity as those of Elias, their spirit is identical.

The charms of St. Theresa as woman and saint, united with her marvelous activities, serve as a cloak to her great austerities and her intimate union with God, and because of this, people readily admit her holiness and dignity without accepting her rigorous way of life. It is the same with St. John of the Cross. They may recognize the solitary penitent and the scholastic exposition of his severe teachings, but fail to recognize him as a man gifted with unusual activity and a heart richly endowed with tender love. Yet the spirit of both is the same. The *Way of Perfection* and the *Interior Castle* of St. Theresa are comparable to the *Ascent of Mount Carmel* and the *Living Flame of Love* of St. John. In one we notice the womanly and saintly traits of St. Theresa, charmingly interwoven with the greatest austerities of religious life; while in the other, the solitary asceticism of St. John cannot entirely conceal the ardor of a man inflamed with the love of God and his fellow men.

Paradoxically, St. Theresa presents virtue as something lovable, easy, and agreeable, while the essential part of her doctrine is an ardent love for sufferings, severity, and penance. There was no attraction for her in this life except in the sufferings she could exchange for the love of God. How well this is portrayed in her own words: "Those who really love God, love all that is good, seek all that is good; praise all that is good, and invariably join forces with the goodness of humanity. Could they hide their love? . . . It will always display itself . . . provided it is a true love of God."[5]

St. John presents himself as the hermetical type, seeking retirement, and placing all his affection in suffering. Yet this ecstatic saint founded and governed many houses of prayer, fostered a missionary spirit among his disciples, and wrote many books which are still leading innumerable souls to a closer union with God. All this is evident from his writings: ". . . devout souls achieve sanctity in many ways, according to the will of God, according to the spirit and height he has reached in perfection, by means of a variety of spiritual works and exercises, literally running along the road to eternal life, which is perfected in the evangelical counsels."[6] So great was St. John's energy that placing all his trust in God, he never knew discouragement. "God is so pleased with the soul filled with hope, who never wearies in its search for Him, that He gives it all it desires."[7]

St. John's famous path to nothing traced on his symbolic mountain, as a means of reaching the summit of perfection, causes fear and discouragement to those who do not completely understand its true meaning. Therefore St. John tells us that this is the very path once trod by the divine Redeemer, a path which He is still treading as the Shepherd of souls, as He continuously searches for the beloved shepherdess, despite the weariness and suffering entailed.

A shepherd, desolate and in grief
Is brooding o'er his loved one.
Alone, uncomforted, disconsolate
His heart well torn with unrequited love.

He weeps, not for some love wound given of yore
For no such thing could grieve him so,
His beautiful shepherdess has forgotten him
He weeps because she thinks of him no more.

And so, because she thinks of him no more
That shepherd-maid of his, so fair to see —
He lets his alien foes treat cruelly
The breast that love has stricken very sore.

Then slowly he climbs when much time is o'er
Into a tree, with fair arms wide outspread
And desirous only for his wanted love
He dies of unrequited love.

The representation of the divine Redeemer in so tender a
manner reveals a heart filled with an ineffable love toward God
and man, not one overcome with austerity and severity. Such a
perfected love proves a tremendous stimulus to all who wish to
serve Christ, for as St. Paul says: "The charity of Christ holdeth
us."[8] While not minimizing the doctrine of Christ, he diligently
cultivates an intimate intercourse with God, knowing well that
man must seek his strength through prayer and close union with
God. The fruit of this communion is the performance of prolific
works of God who is served in the person of His creatures.

It was the same love of prayer and suffering that induced St.
Theresa to begin the reform of Carmel: "I served the Lord with
my poor prayers, persuading the sisters to work zealously for the
increase and sanctification of His Church. In this I found the
satisfaction of my greatest desires."[9] It was her earnest wish, then,
that the fruit of our prayers and penances should be the desire of
doing good to all as the following incident shows: "A Franciscan
friar, Fray Alonso Maldonado, recently returned from the Indies
has the same desire as I for the salvation of souls, only he was able
to do something about it. He discussed the millions of souls
perishing for want of knowledge of God and incited us to mortification and penance on their behalf. I was so distressed by the loss of
so many souls that I wept bitterly, imploring our Lord that my

prayers might be of some avail, since I had nothing more to give for souls. How I envied those who could spend their lives ministering to others for the love of God, even though in so doing they might suffer a thousand deaths! Yet the realization of the numberless souls who have been saved by the prayers and sacrifices of those who never knew actual martyrdom filled me with even greater zeal. Thus our Lord gave me to understand that He prizes one soul, which in His mercy is saved through our prayers, than all other services we can render to Him."[10]

The vigorous Carmelite spirit is formulated by a great austerity and ineffable sweetness, a spirit commenced by Elias and continued in all the Carmelite saints, acquiring its perfection in St. Theresa and St. John of the Cross. This Carmelite spirit is meant to endure through all generations, to be appropriated by austere men as well as by delicate virgins. Consequently it must contain in itself something immutable which is its essence, and something which simultaneously is so mutable that it can be readily adapted to all different classes of peoples, nations, and time. It follows then that whatever must be adapted for specified times and circumstances can and should be modified by legitimate authority according to the necessity which arises. To fail to do this would entail fatal consequences for any religious institute, for it would be to mistake the immutable and essential for the circumstantial and mutable, rendering the work of its subjects inefficacious. It must be remembered that an institute, despite the fact that its origin is from God, depends upon human energy for its activity.

It is the essentials, then, that are contained in the Admonitions of St. John of the Cross. If one meditates frequently upon them, he comes to realize the necessity of practicing each admonition for the acquisition of solid virtue and the evangelical perfections. At the same time, however, they are so flexible that they can be applied to any religious, regardless of the circumstances of time, place, and occupation. The strong and invigorating elements of the Carmelite religious spirit found in these Admonitions are applicable for all religious men and women, Tertiaries, and even seculars who are lovers of perfection. "He who practises the following instructions is freed from the hindrances of all creatures of the world, and is defended from the wiles and deceits of the devil."[11] It is not sufficient to observe some of these counsels and neglect others, since the enemies against whom they are directed cannot be conquered separately. "In order to conquer any one of these three enemies, it is necessary to conquer all of them; if one is weakened, so are the other two; when all are conquered there remains no more warfare in the soul."[12] There is no circumstance, then, in life wherein one or other of these admonitions may not be applied. Blessed is he who "takes them well to heart" for without any other practises or exercises of virtue he will soon attain perfect peace of soul. To use the words of St. John, "He will enjoy the peaceful refreshment of the Holy Ghost."[13]

Religious loving the teachings of St. John and desirous of practicing them will accommodate themselves to any place, occupation, or character, realizing that any contradictions which present themselves are excellent opportunities of overcoming self-love. The continued observance of religious observance with all its monotony is another occasion for sacrifices, which though small in themselves, are most pleasing to God. In his spiritual and social relations with his neighbor the remembrance of these counsels renders the religious' work more apostolic. Then neither the vain adulations of the rich, nor the often unpleasant contacts with the poor, will be able to withdraw him from his duty; there will be no false pride in his success, no envy at the achievements of another, no depression in failure and contradictions.

For those seeking a high degree of contemplation, these admonitions serve as a counterbalance, lest they become lost in a fantastic world. Those who never deviate from the simplicity and monotony of a regular and obscure life need them as a preventative from falling into weariness and despondency. For those ordinarily employed in external works, they are a powerful reminder to live within the sanctuary of their own hearts, lest, according to the expression of St. Paul, ". . . they become as sounding brass or a tinkling cymbal."[14] Anyone, then, who takes these admonitions seriously, not deviating from the path marked out by them, will be able to unfold all the energies of his spirit with great benefit to both himself and his neighbor. He will work faithfully and purely for God, bearing within himself the fullness of grace. "A good work performed for the love of God, in purity and singleness of heart, increases the kingdom of God within oneself."[15]

No trial, however difficult, can present itself, which will not find a solution in one of these admonitions. St. John considers them so necessary that he tells us that without them we cannot obtain true peace of soul. In times of temptation it is well to meditate on these words of St. John, "Why do you complain, my son? Why are your devotions and occupations insipid to you? Why do you find this companion so trying? Is it because your self-love has been wounded? All these mortifications should be borne with humility and inward patience. Have you forgotten that this was your purpose in entering religion? That thus you might be humbled and mortified so you might possess eternal life? If this was not your intention, then it would have profited you more to have remained in the world, seeking your own praise and satisfaction."[16] Exterior austerities combined with interior sweetness, then, is the sound spirituality preached by St. Theresa and St. John of the Cross and handed down to their posterity.

Men of great prayer, who were gifted with the spirit of enterprise, emulated perfectly the spirit of their holy founders, filled the deserts as penitents while at the same time they extended their apostolic zeal and missionary spirit to the entire world by their prolific writings. All this is exemplified in the lives of such venerable fathers as Jerome Gratian, Thomas of Jesus, Peter of the Mother of God, John of Jesus, Dominic of Jesus and Mary, and countless others. Their penance and interior recollection were in perfect harmony with their great zeal and they have left an indelible mark on the world. The reform of Carmel has passed through many vicissitudes during the past two centuries. Political disturbances and misinterpretation of St. John's doctrine have done more harm to Carmel than to any other religious order. Yet despite the adversity of the times, the works of St. Theresa and St. John are still being revived with admirable freshness and vigor. Throughout the world may be found the children of these two great reformers who by their prayer and example are bringing great glory to God and His blessed Mother.

Divine Providence has blessed our own day with one of the most delicate flowers of the Carmelite garden. A materialistic world, which despite its deviation from what is right feels a strong desire for genuine spirituality, is never tired of admiring the Little Flower of Jesus. From ample experience and knowledge we do not exaggerate when we say that there are many beautiful flowers to be found throughout the many gardens of Carmel. That Divine Providence conceals them from the gaze of the world does not lessen their intrinsic holiness. There is little that is extraordinary about the "Little Flower of Jesus." Rather she is the perfect exemplification of the teachings of Carmel's great saints. Divesting her of the accouterments which form the basis of her charm for many, let us study her interior life and fundamental thoughts which are a genuine expression of her conscience and personality. It is evident that they radiate the doctrine of St. John of the Cross to whom she was greatly devoted: ". . . I drew much light from the works of St. John of the Cross . . . for a long period of time his writings were the only food of my soul."[17] This is verified in her writings, for substantially her "letters" and "Poetry" contain the doctrine of the "Ascent of Mount Carmel" and the "Counsels" well meditated on and perfectly lived.

Despite the great austerities of the Order vocations are not lacking in the present day. Hundreds of young men and women, with vigorous mind and ardent heart, guided by these ascetic admonitions, sustain and increase what was commenced by the early reformers, opening up new horizons throughout the world. It would be well for all Carmelites to assimilate what is contained in the "Counsels" thus safeguarding their activities and energies in perfect harmony with the spirit of St. John and resulting in the greater glory of God and their own sanctification.

But the doctrines of St. John are not exclusively for Carmelites; they are applicable to any religious, since there is not one counsel among them which cannot be practiced most expediently by every religious person in whatever circumstance of life. They may also serve as the guiding light for Tertiaries who desire to live according to the rule of life propounded in these wise maxims. It is evident then, that these counsels, like all works of great merit, are of universal application.

Synthesizing the "Counsels" we find that the spirit of obedience to authority or to superiors, without consideration of their personal qualifications, is an absolute necessity for peace and perfect harmony, not only in religious houses but in society in general. Such perfect submission is not degrading, but rather ennobles and dignifies a man, because he is not subjecting himself to the whims of an equal, but to the dictates of his own conscience. This subjection results in the greatest and most pure type of humility, which is necessary to overcome the wiles of the devil.

Character differences among individuals render all social life difficult. St. John teaches us how to overcome this enemy of harmony among men by considering these differences of character as the most excellent and efficacious means, supplied by Divine Providence, to help us in our personal sanctification. Such a spirit of self-abnegation and sacrifice would insure the greatest social peace.

Finally in the last two counsels St. John instructs us to accept sufferings joyfully, even arriving at the point of seeking them as means sent by God for our closer union with Him.

Thus these celebrated admonitions of St. John are a marvelous compendium of useful doctrines, which all persons in any religious congregation will find helpful for personal sanctification and the salvation of souls.

CHAPTER TWENTY-ONE

AGAIN—THE BASIC VIRTUES

No one can deny that the teachings of St. John of the Cross reveal a soul completely filled with the love of God and possessed of the beautiful ideal of sanctity which, while in complete conformity to the Gospel, simultaneously reveals a profound knowledge of the inconsistency of human nature.

When a doctrine is propounded which deflates egoism and appears to restrict our beloved liberty it is very human to find many reasons for not putting it into practice. If we cannot deny its truth or justice, nor the excellence of its objectives, we invent a multitude of reasons and arguments to convince ourselves that although such a doctrine would be most admirable for the saints it is not at all applicable to our circumstances. Recently the Church placed St. John among the doctors of the Church thus publicly recognizing and clearly approving the teachings of the humble solitary of Duruelo. The deep questions of mystical theology which he explains in so incomparable a manner have been revealed to very few persons. Since this is true it might appear that the importance of his work should be limited to an appreciation of these mysteries instead of being actually applied to daily living. To refute this implication the saint takes the greatest care to explain the class of people to whom he dedicates his work. "It is not my intention to speak to everyone but rather with those persons of our primitive Carmel, both friars and nuns whom God in His mercy has called to a high degree of sacred mysticism."[1]

This leads to the question, "Does the severe religious aceticism set forth in the counsels and formulated by a saint enamored of solitude still remain applicable to the present day whose circumstances differ considerably from those of the period when these counsels were written?" Disregarding circumstances, it still remains that these admonitions were written for contemplatives and those aspiring to contemplation, thus containing a doctrine which is both ascetical and mystical. "The religious who wishes to arrive at holy sanctity, silence and self abnegation, as well as a poverty of spirit which will enable him to gaze peacefully on the presence of God dwelling with himself, must free himself completely from every creature of this world, defending himself against the attacks of the devil and exerting every possible effort to overcome his greatest enemy, himself. This, of necessity is the result of the following teachings."[2] It would be a dangerous thing then, for any religious to think that such admonitions did not apply to him. These wise precautions remain just as applicable in the present day, after a lapse of four centuries, as they were in the lifetime of the saint, formulating a code which is absolutely indispensable to sanctity and evangelical perfection. All those who meditate on these admonitions will marvel at the logic which they contain. The saint does not enter into long discussions but goes straight to the core of evangelical perfection which is the possession of peace of soul, ". . . interior silence, complete self-abnegation, and poverty of spirit, clarifies the vision of God within us and unites us completely to God."[3]

With the wisdom of a profound observer he plumbs the depths of human nature and formulates wise cautions for everyone so that, despite his multiple weaknesses, he can follow the divine command, "Take up thy cross, daily, and follow Me."[4] ". . . Be you therefore perfect, as also your heavenly Father is perfect."[5] More than that, he reveals the cures for human weaknesses. It is clear that Christian asceticism directed thus toward vacillating human nature has to be equally flexible in its fundamental demands and restrictions. What remains indispensable and unchangeable is the doctrine of Christ Himself. "For there is one God and one mediator . . . Jesus Christ, yesterday, and today, and the same forever."[6] Thus He and He alone can be the ideal of all our aspirations, the model for our imitation, and the unfailing Fountain from which we receive all the graces necessary to follow the road which leads to eternal life. If we forget that we are weak and seek our consolation elsewhere than in Christ, we are guilty of self-deception and merit nothing in the sight of God. If, however, we are guided by Christ in all our actions, we shall arrive at the very portals of eternity, for, as the evangelist says, "He is the gateway and there is no other entrance into eternal life."[7] Completely in accord with this doctrine, is the teaching of St. John which, if followed, will assuredly merit eternal life: "Let your first care be to imitate Christ in all His works, studying to perform each one of them in the manner Christ, Himself, would have used."[8] If, then, these teachings are fundamental (and they are), then they are absolutely necessary for the personal sanctification of each individual. These basic teachings can be reduced to three: faith, sacrifice, and charity. We need faith to guide all the actions of our lives, sacrifice to sustain and nourish us, and charity in order to overcome the hardships met with on the road to perfection.

Primarily, we need a strong spirit of faith which will enable us to see Divine Providence in all things, even the most insignificant. We know from the Gospel that God our Father has a tender, loving solicitude for us, looking upon each of us as His beloved son.[9] We ought likewise to believe that He who has numbered the very hairs of our heads[10] will permit nothing to happen to us which is not for His greater glory and our own sanctification. In order to deepen and vivify this faith we ought to often repeat the wonderful words of resignation, "Thy will be done." This short phrase contains all that is necessary for Christian and religious perfection, namely, complete conformity to the will of God.

When a person understands the meaning of "Thy will be done" and lives in accordance with this realization, he recognizes the workings of Divine Providence in every circumstance of life, despite the difficulties which might present themselves. For such a person, his thoughts, actions, and desires are completely conformed to faith because it is only with a deep spirit of faith that one can recognize the workings of Divine Providence in all the events of human life to such an extent that he is able to say to God with the complete abandonment of a child, "Lord, Thy Will be done. I desire only that which Thou willest. I love this because it is Your Will and I accept it willingly."

Joined with this great virtue of faith is the indispensable spirit of sacrifice. The same loving Savior who guides all our actions tells us that for those who would be His true disciples the cross is a necessary element, which must be carried daily in order to follow Him. The way of the cross is the only way which true lovers of Christ can choose, and it is found all around us, in the inclemencies of the weather, in the idiosyncrasies of those with whom we dwell, with our own constant failings and weaknesses. God permits us to be surrounded by sorrows which frequently bring us to our knees, seeking His aid, so we will not cling to the things of the world. Wisdom looks through tear dimmed eyes to the beauty of the celestial world.

It would be totally useless to try to avoid crosses either directly or indirectly because to do so only increases our sufferings and makes them more intolerable. It would likewise be renouncing the ideal of religious perfection that Christ has commanded all who love Him to pursue. Yet even faith and suffering are not sufficient. They both must be strengthened and supported by the greatest virtue of all, namely charity. Without this mysterious and divine unction which our Divine Savior reserves for His dearest friends, all the crosses and sufferings which surround us would be unbearable. We would falter along the way and never reach the heights of perfection incumbent on us because of our religious profession. If we were to accept the greatest sufferings without a true spirit of charity, we will never arrive at the state of divine union to which we have been called and all our works are worthless in the sight of God, who accepts our works and measures their worth in proportion to the love with which they were performed. It is totally impossible, then, for any religious to attempt to construct a spiritual edifice on any other basis than the triple spirit of faith, sacrifice, and charity because this was the foundation given by Christ Himself.

St. Paul tells us that there are many diverse methods of arriving at sanctification. Some may build with gold, silver, and other precious metals; others may use simple mortar, while still others are content to use the cheapest materials they can find. But when these materials are exposed to the elements then they show their true worth; exposed to the fire of temptation the cheaper materials are destroyed while the same fires only cleanse and purify the worthwhile. Even the most rudimentary knowledge, then, of these virtues is sufficient to make us realize that the only things of real value in the eyes of God are the works and prayers that have been supported by faith, charity, and sacrifice since these form the essential basis of evangelical perfection. There is a greater guarantee of immortality to the works fostered by these virtues and a greater assurance of a more powerful resistance to the inconstancies of human nature which are always diametrically opposed to the beautiful ideals of evangelical sanctity. All these truths have been admirably set forth for our study and imitation by the author of the *Imitation of Christ*.

This same universal application has been adapted to the circumstances of all times in the teachings of St. John of the Cross. His "Counsels" are a marvelous compendium of the ascetical doctrine of the spirit of faith, love, and sacrifice which should motivate the life of every religious. The most admirable thing is that they are not only a condensation of evangelical holiness but they are an equally detailed application to the varied circumstances involved in religious vocations. St. John exhorts all his sons and disciples to the practice of a pure and simple faith which marks the first steps on the road to perfection, and ultimately leads to the heights of the mystical mountain of Carmel where souls are transformed by their intimate union with God. Once this union is complete, souls experience even here on this earth some of the ineffable joys which will consume them hereafter.

Well has St. John been called the "Doctor of Faith" because he has placed his trust not in marvelous discourses or divine revelations but rather in an acceptance of the practicality of the mysteries of the Trinity and all theology which can result in nothing but a sane ascetical religion. This same spirit of faith permeates the purgation of contemplatives as explained in "The Ascent of Mount Carmel" as well as their complete purification treated of in "The Dark Night of the Soul."

It is precisely this spirit of faith that recognizes in every event the paternity and wisdom of Divine Providence, which permits all things for all greater sanctification. According to St. John these mortifications are to be found in our fellow men, who are nothing but the refining tools of a loving God. The superiors, who govern us, are simply the representatives of God and nothing more. God does not wish us to obey them because of their personal merits or qualifications but simply because they are taking His place. Such a sincere subjection and submission is not possible without a deep spirit of faith and a practical belief in the mysteries of the Incarnation and the Trinity since it is very difficult to see in the disposition and actions of men a reflection of the love and wisdom of

Divine Providence arranged for our sanctification. All this is naturally difficult because it conflicts with our spirit of pride which would refuse to recognize the presence of Divine Providence in the minutest details of our lives. For this reason St. John firmly bases his doctrine on the virtue of faith.

Combined with the spirit of faith must be the spirit of sacrifice in all our actions. Self-abnegation in all things, without a desire for either human or divine consolation, leaving all to the will of God, believing of ourselves, we are nothing but weakness and imperfection and that without a severe and practical asceticism we cannot arrive at the heights of perfection. If the saint, in the first steps of purgation in his famous "Ascent of Mount Carmel," wrote of the necessity of a total abnegation of self in both the human and the divine, he emphasizes this same doctrine in the "Counsels" where he urges us never to seek our own pleasure but rather to accept what is most humbling, even arriving at the point of deliberately seeking for this. "To be despised and regarded as worthless" was the doctrine of St. John of the Cross. Such a doctrine surpasses human heroism, eradicates all pride and is the test of true mystical love.

The true spirit of charity radiates throughout the pages of this incomparable master of evangelical perfection. It would be impossible to continue in faith or self-abnegation if a deep spirit of charity did not enlighten the shadows lurking on the road to perfection. The saint knew well that blind faith without love is impossible, that nothing is permanent, that no one thing can completely satisfy the heart except a love such as the love of God for the human heart. Every human being has a great longing for love and affection and we are very incredulous on this point especially if we have been deceived. In order to receive the affection of others it is necessary that we first show them a spirit of benevolence, loving them despite the faults or failings which we might recognize in our dealings with them. St. John of the Cross tells us "Where there is no love, put love, and there will be love."

This thought contains the doctrine of St. John relative to charity. If we wish to be loved, then we must love; we must overlook the weaknesses of others; we must be willing to accept the greater part of the burden realizing that others will love us only in proportion as we go out of ourselves to show our love for them. All this reflects the love of Christ for all men whom He loved infinitely, accepting them as they were, and overlooking their faults. "Judge not, and you shall not be judged."[11] St. John demands, then, a great respect for the written law, especially the law of charity, urging us to bring charity to the places where it does not exist. This faithful, filial submission to authority and to superiors is a fulfilling of the law of Christ, "Do unto others as you would have them do unto you."[12] Surely, there would be perfect peace in religious families if this doctrine were perfectly observed. One of the greatest missions we have is that of bringing peace and charity to religious houses where it may be lacking.

This doctrine of charity is just as important and applicable today as it was when it was first written by St. John; moreover, it will always be a fundamental obligation of all those who aspire to religious perfection.

These three admonitions of St. John concerning faith, sacrifice, and charity are the synthesis of a beautiful ideal, which will infallibly lead man to overcome the principal difficulties he is bound to encounter in his struggle toward the eternal goal.

CHAPTER TWENTY-TWO

THE PERFECTION OF CHARITY

If the precautions recommended by St. John of the Cross in the "Counsels" are indispensable for the religious for whom he wrote them, then they are equally applicable and practicable for any religious regardless of time or circumstance. Although God has surrounded the religious vocation with innumerable graces by means of which eminent sanctity could be obtained, the current spirit of materialism acts as a powerful threat to its achievement. Since the teachings of St. John are directed toward a realization of the dangers of excessive liberties in both spiritual and temporal matters, the ascetical doctrine which he advocates has a special application in the present day. Living as we do in an era of speed, it is comparatively easy to become indifferent regarding readings which require much thought and meditation. Thus we seek the impetus needed for a deeper spirituality in the condensations of the greater spiritual writers. It is precisely in this condensation that the merit of the "Counsels" of St. John of the Cross lies. The form is abbreviated and yet the richness of material is such that not many pages have been covered before one has discovered the core of spirituality applicable to any religious, active or contemplative, regardless of the circumstances which surround his life. It is in his works that we find that all the wisdom of the world and human ability, compared with the infinite wisdom of God, are simple ignorance; all the wealth and glory of all creatures in comparison with the wealth which is God, is supreme poverty. This comprises the evaluation of Christianity which it is not easy for modern man to accept. Thus there are some, who after reading works on mystical theology, are convinced that the era in which they live is not conducive to the same sanctity possible in other periods. Such reasoning is both lamentable and illogical. The saints and all great servants of God bear eloquent testimony to the fact that sanctity is not a question of time or circumstance. With Ecclesiasticus we can say, "From the beginning and before the world, was I created, and unto the world to come I shall not cease to be . . . and my abode is in the full assembly of saints."[1]

The combat between good and evil, truth and dishonesty is both universal and perpetual, because the devil who hates God vents his hatred upon all human nature, and will continue to do so until the end of time when the final decisive battle will overcome all evil. It is natural, therefore, to find that in some places and at some times the good supersedes the evil and vice versa, since such fluctuations are accidental to time and circumstance. The tremendous struggle between good and evil, between divine grace, which may intimately unite us with God, and the inclination to evil, which may completely separate us from Him, is the same for every human being, because it is the same enemy which all mankind must eventually face and overcome. It is evident then that the perfect practice of evangelical counsels or severe asceticism always presents many difficulties regardless of time, place, or circumstance.

Briefly studying the pros and cons, the beauty and dangers of religious spirit in the present days we find that immorality is not the most dangerous and powerful opposition against which religious have to fight; nor can it be termed the most characteristic phenomenon of our age since a study of history proves the contrary. Rather, the outstanding and most common characteristic today is the widespread spirit of indifferentism, found in both the secular and religious life. The indifferent religious, who may believe himself to be a true follower of Christ and Catholicism, is the cause of the greatest amount of damage that can befall the religious spirit. The mere practice of Christianity or a few devout practices of prayer and mortification without serious reflection or depth of meaning constitute the danger, which is known as indifferentism, because such a person is seeking himself and not God. Such materialism does not seek to know the causes or motives influencing human nature and is content with surface knowledge of the great mysteries of faith which should form the guiding influences of our lives.

Living, as many do, on the surface of things, they fail to penetrate the depths of the great doctrines of faith which should be the guide of their consciences. It is a fear of God rather than the love of God which becomes the motivating force of their actions so that while they are not sinful, yet they are not as meritorious in His eyes as they should be. Thus, in a materialistic sense, we live in a more or less routine manner being subtly influenced by the worldly spirit which surrounds them. It naturally follows that living in such a weak spirit of faith generates an equally shallow interior spirit, since religious life, even though it may be engaged in higher functions, tends to reflect its surrounding circumstances and times.

Yet it is solely for the purpose of living in the world but not of its spirit that God has called souls to the religious life expecting that by their total consecration each one will strive to reform himself interiorly, not according to the spirit of the world in which he lives but "to perfect himself by knowing and doing what is most conformable to the holy will of God."[2] Without this interior reformation it is impossible for any religious vocation to be all that God intended it to be. It is evident that this interior growth in spirituality is in proportion to the difficulties overcome and as the contradictions imperceptibly infiltrated into the soul by the world which surrounds it are conquered.

Morally speaking each one is the product of what he reads and discusses. Since the spirit as well as the body grows in accordance with that with which it is nurtured, it follows that what is read and discussed have a decided influence on one's interior life. The more profound and meditative the works a person will pursue, the more closely his soul will become identified with truth. It is lamentable, then, that many of the readings and conversations, even of religious, are permeated with the spirit of the world rather than the spirit of truth. Therefore, today, even more than before it is necessary that a religious seek a more solid and perfect means of enriching his spiritual life, by provocative thought and meditative readings. So firmly rooted should a religious become in truth and spirituality that even the strongest wiles and suggestions of the evil one will be unable to undermine this progress on the road to perfection. A soul permeated with the teachings of Christ and living in accordance with them will radiate Christ in the world which He has redeemed, regardless of the spirit of indifferentism which may fill it. "For what was impossible to the law, God has made good.[3] For . . . neither death, nor life, . . . nor any other creature shall be able to separate us from the love of God, which is in Christ Jesus."[4]

There can be found no interior reformation, wiser, more profound, more complete, and yet more flexible than the admonitions
of St. John of the Cross. Its wisdom and profundity directly attacks
the roots of human weaknesses from which proceed the obstacles
man has to overcome in his struggle to achieve sanctity. It is
complete because it strikes directly at self-love, pride, and sensuality
and uncovers the wiles and deceits of the devil. At the same time
it is completely flexible because it can be both adjusted and adapted
to fit the needs of all regardless of time or circumstance.

These counsels do not contain the practice of severe penances
which might intimidate weaker souls. Nor do they propound a
psychological or intellectual doctrine which the less educated would
find difficult to interpret and understand. What the saint does
exact is a complete internal reformation, possible to everyone,
because of its reasonableness, logic, and complete conformity to
evangelical counsels. "While engaged in manual or intellectual
pursuits, all should strive continually to lift their hearts to Christ,
having that as their chief concern, and to burn with perfect love
of Him."[5] The absolute necessity for all vocations, then, is to seek
to serve God in secret, completely hidden from the eyes of the
world; seeking neither its honors nor its acclamations while exteriorly engaged in a glorious apostolate of doing the will of God.
It is only in this complete submission to the will of God, performing
all our works and actions for His greater honor and glory that
according to St. John we will ". . . arrive at peace and joy in the
holy Spirit, a complete unity with God, and we shall actually run
along the road to perfection."[6] In this is the plentiful realization of
the beautiful ideal of perfection which our Savior taught and which
every saint has endeavored to live with absolute fidelity. One who
follows the admonitions of St. John can be reasonably assured, then,
of attaining sanctity and eternal happiness. On the other hand, if
we neglect these counsels ". . . you will not be a true religious . . .
how many religious have failed to realize the fulness of their
vocation . . . and how little value their obedience has in the eyes
of God."[7]

Many religious today live only superficially both in their knowledge of spiritual things and their practice. For some religious
practices are tempered with social conveniences, for others they are
no more than a matter of mere sentiment. They are inconstant

in fulfilling their daily religious obligations, at times omitting them entirely. Such religious are not guided by conscience, do not bring any glory to God, and contribute nothing to the general spiritual welfare of their neighbors. Nothing could be more contrary to the doctrine taught by St. John. Such a method of living directly opposes the teaching: "To desire the greater honor and glory of God in all things . . . to desire the sufferings of Christ rather than worldly glory . . . Christ is little known because those who claim to be His friends seek His consolations rather than His sufferings. . . ."[8] It is apparent, then, that one of the most distinctive and alarming characteristics of the religious spirit today is the number of good persons, who have vowed a total consecration, yet who are living only a superficial interior life. In a more deplorable manner, the doctrine of the saints, which in its very essence is spiritual, is being interpreted in a purely material way. It is precisely to remedy this evil that the admonitions of St. John are to be accounted as invaluable in the present day. Religion, which in many instances, both secular and religious, has become a doctrine of self-complacency and personal standards needs to be reinforced with the doctrine of St. John in all its severity, its complete self-renunciation, and an entrance into a superhuman world which is absolutely out of proportion with our present standards.

St. John, faithful to the apostolic tradition, sees the whole of our natural life directed toward the perfection of charity and transformation into the love of God. Contemplation, then, is not an end in itself, rather it is directed toward a closer union with God. "There is no better and more necessary work than love."[9] Hence, it is love itself that gives rise to contemplation by the supernatural bond of charity which brings us into intimate relation with the Trinity. Since this love is derived from faith, which unites our intellect with the profundity of the Deity, we are bound to affirm that a living faith, enlightened by the gifts of the Holy Spirit and informed with charity, is the fundamental principle of mystical experience and the sole "Proximate and proportionate means of divine union."[10] St. John of the Cross is never wearied of repeating this truth.

There is no more violent distortion than that which would make St. John an intellectualist in search of a refined form of knowledge. What he desired for himself and for his followers was suffering and contempt for the sake of Him whom he loved. His spiritual doctrine is not a metaphysical dogma but rather evangelical, filled with nothingness, emptiness, and complete renouncement of self and all that might draw him away from the Beloved. To abide in utter spiritual poverty "is the soul's absolute duty" according to the Son of God. "If any man come to me, and hate not . . . his own life, he cannot be my disciple."[11]

St. John addresses his "Counsels" to souls who are willing to pay the price demanded by the practical rigor of the Gospel, which is not a mere external detachment but a radical internal one, a complete renunciation of proprietorship in and of, the purely natural exercise of our emotions making them live by a higher love. As the soul cannot attain the highest degree of charity unless it loves itself in and for God and is completely subordinated to supernatural charity, so it cannot take even the first steps on this road unless it is willing to make this interior sacrifice in its fullest meanings.

In the general framework of human society each one of us is called upon to add to his own weakness the burden of heroism and to do this we need the most rigorous secrets of wisdom and strength. With all the weight of misunderstood love, the cross weighs heavy today upon a materialistic world and those who are enlightened by the doctrine of St. John of the Cross must be willing to pass through the "nakedness of spirit" in order to advance on the road to perfection.

If there are some who cannot fully understand the doctrine of St. John and because of this misinterpretation create a counterfeit mysticism for themselves which is utterly worthless in the eyes of God, there are other souls who attempt to follow him in his fundamental teaching: "To be despised and regarded as worthless." What distinguishes the true mystic from all others is the way he is attracted not by penances and self-imposed physical sufferings, but rather by the insatiable thirst for humiliations which end in complete annihilation of self. A teaching such as this eradicates all pride, and surpasses human heroism, passing into the "darkness of the cross" there to taste of the "inexhaustible depths of the Wisdom and knowledge of God" which is the perfection of charity.

FOOTNOTES

Notes for Chapter One

1 Acts 19:13.
2 *Ibid.*, 15:16.
3 Rom. 2:21.
4 Ps. 49:16, 17.
5 *Life of St. Theresa*, XXXI:17.
6 Mt. 5:48.
7 Jn. 14:2.
8 Cf. Phil. 3:17.
9 *Life of St. Theresa*, XXXVI:29.
10 *Ibid.*
11 *Ibid.*, XXXVIII:24.
12 *Relations of St. Theresa*, XIV.
13 3 Jn. 1:11.
14 St. John of the Cross, *Advisos* (Book of Counsels to Religious), a. 69.
15 Exod. 25:40.
16 Cf. Isa. 51:2.
17 Mt. 10:39.
18 Gal. 5:6.

Notes for Chapter Two

1 *La Santidad en el Claustro*, Padre Lucas, II, 22.
2 *Ascent of Mt. Carmel*, John of Cross, II, 11.
3 *Advisos: aviso* 7, 8, 9.
4 *La Santidad*, II, 33.
5 *Ibid.*, 37.
6 *Ibid.*, 38.
7 *Ascent of Mt. Carmel*, I, 40.
8 Mt. 7:14.

Notes for Chapter Three

1 *La Santidad*, III, 40.
2 *Ibid.*, 41.
3 *Ibid.*, 43.
4 Cf. 1 Cor. 9:19, 20.
5 Letter to M. Catalina.
6 Letter VII to Juana de Pedraza.
7 Letter XIII to Juana de Pedraza.
8 Cf. Mt. 10:37; Lk. 14:26.
9 1 Jn. 4:7, 8.
10 1 Jn. 2:10, 11.
11 Jn. 13:34.
12 Cf. *Ibid.*
13 *Ascent of Mt. Carmel*, III, XIX, 1, 5.
14 Cf. 2 Cor. 3:6, 11.
15 *Relations of St. Theresa*, II, XLVI.

NOTES FOR CHAPTER FOUR

1 *Spiritual Canticle*, St. John of Cross, Canticle XIX.
2 Letter X to M. Maria of Jesus.
3 *Avisos:* aviso 27, 28.
4 1 Jn. 4:20.
5 1 Cor. 13, 7.
6 *Avisos:* aviso 184, 185, 186.
7 *Ibid.*, 127, 152.
8 *Interior Castle*, St. Theresa, III, 8.
9 *Conceptions of Divine Love*, St. John of Cross, VI, 13.
10 *Ascent of Mt. Carmel*, III, XXII, 1.
11 *Avisos:* aviso 118.
12 Rom. 1:31.
13 *Avisos:* aviso 161.
14 *Interior Castle*, VIII, 261.
15 Jn. 13:34.
16 *Ibid.*, 35.
17 Rom. 13:8, 10.
18 Cf. 2 Cor. 2:15.

NOTES FOR CHAPTER FIVE

1 *La Santidad* IV, 98.
2 *Summa Theol.*, II–II, q. XLXXXVI, a. 7.
3 *Avisos:* aviso 2.
4 *Ibid.:* aviso 69.
5 Gen. 1:28.
6 *Prayer of an enamored soul*, St. John of the Cross.
7 Gen. 1:28.
8 Lk. 6:24.
9 Mt. 19:24.
10 Mt. 5:3, 4, 8.
11 Mt. 6:26, 28–30, 32, 33.
12 *Ascent of Mt. Carmel*, I, III, 4, 10.
13 *Avisos:* aviso 215.
14 Letter X to Sr. Maria of Jesus.

NOTES FOR CHAPTER SIX

1 Cf. James 1:26.
2 *La Santidad*, VI, 117.
3 *Ibid.*, 120.
4 *Avisos:* aviso 4.
5 1 Pet. 5:8.
6 Lk. 22:31, 32.
7 *Dark Night of the Soul*, XXIII, 5.
8 Cf. Ps. 118:71.
9 Cf. Ecclus. 34:9.
10 1 Cor. 10:12.
11 Prov. 24:15, 16.
12 Cf. Jn. 15:16.
13 St. Bernard on Religious Perfection.

NOTES FOR CHAPTER SEVEN

[1] *La Santidad*, VIII, 136.
[2] James 1:26.
[3] *Summa Theol.*, II–II, q. LX, 23.
[4] *Ibid.*
[5] Rom. 2:1.
[6] 1 Cor. 4:5.
[7] Lk. 6:37, 38.
[8] Wisd. 12:18, 19.
[9] Mt. 12, 34.
[10] Cf. Ecclus. 37:21.
[11] 2 Cor. 3:6.
[12] *La Santidad* VII, 152.
[13] Jn. 13:34.
[14] 2 Cor. 2:15, 16.

NOTES FOR CHAPTER EIGHT

[1] Mt. 13:39.
[2] Eph. 6:11.
[3] Apoc. 12:9, 10, 12, 17.
[4] *Summa Theol.*, I, q. CXIV, a. 2.
[5] 2 Tim. 4:8.
[6] Apoc. 3:11.
[7] Cf. Apoc. 3:21.
[8] Acts 10:38.
[9] *Ascent of Mt. Carmel*, II: X: 4.
[10] *Ibid.*, XIX:6.
[11] *Avisos:* aviso 339.

NOTES FOR CHAPTER NINE

[1] *La Santidad*, IX:124.
[2] Prov. 15:28.
[3] *Avisos:* aviso 243.
[4] Gen. 22:18.
[5] Jn. 14:30, 31.
[6] *Avisos:* aviso 36.
[7] Jer. 2:20.
[8] Cf. Lk. 22:42.
[9] Rom. 5:19.
[10] Jn. 8:43, 44.
[11] Mt. 12:48–50.
[12] Ecclus. 3:1.
[13] Prov. 21:28.
[14] *La Santidad*, IX:176.
[15] Isa. 58:3.
[16] *Dark Night of the Soul*, VI:365.
[17] *Way of Perfection*, XVIII:7.

18 *Avisos:* aviso 4.
19 *Foundations,* V:10.
20 *Avisos:* aviso 10.
21 Cf. 1 Kings 15:23.
22 Jer. 11:20.
23 *Avisos:* aviso 242.
24 *Ascent of Mt. Carmel,* III.

NOTES FOR CHAPTER TEN

1 Phil. 2:8.
2 Apoc. 3:15, 16.
3 Jn. 15:16.
4 Mt. 25:28–30.
5 *Avisos:* aviso 252.
6 *Avisos:* aviso 284.
7 *Way of Perfection,* XXXVI:3, 4, 5.

NOTES FOR CHAPTER ELEVEN

1 *La Santidad,* XI:202.
2 Lk. 10:16.
3 1 Tim. 5:17.
4 Ecclus. 32:1.
5 1 Cor. 6:12.
6 Jn. 21:16, 17.
7 Ps. 39:13.
8 Ps. 5:3, 12–14.
9 Num. 11:11, 12.
10 Ezek. 34:1, 2–4, 7, 10.
11 Isa. 3:4.
12 Hebr. 13:17.
13 Wisd. 6:6.
14 *Life of St. Theresa,* XXXVIII:26.
15 *Ibid.,* 28.

NOTES FOR CHAPTER TWELVE

1 *Avisos:* aviso 10.
2 *Summa Theol.,* II–II, q. CLXXXVI, a. 10.
3 *Ibid.,* II–II, q. CLXXXVI, a. 5.
4 *Ibid.,* II–II, q. CLXXXVI, a. 10.
5 Mt. 5:20, 46–48.
6 Mt. 7:21.
7 *Fundaciones,* V:10.
8 *La Santidad,* XII:244.
9 Cf. Ecclus. 20:11.
10 Letter, St. John Cross, to Mother Leonor Bautista.

Notes for Chapter Thirteen

[1] Mt. 6:1, 3, 16, 18.
[2] Mt. 10:40, 42.
[3] Gen. 3:5.
[4] Lk. 17:1, 2.
[5] *Avisos:* aviso 161, 162.
[6] *La Santidad*, XIII:259.
[7] Lk. 2:51.
[8] Mt. 26:39.
[9] Lk. 9:23.
[10] Jn. 13:15.

Notes for Chapter Fourteen

[1] *Avisos:* aviso 263.
[2] *Dark Night of the Soul*, St. John of Cross, XIX, 3.
[3] *Interior Castle*, X, 7.
[4] *Life of St. Theresa*, XIX, 2.
[5] *Ibid.*, X, 4, 5.
[6] Mt. 25:24–26.
[7] Mt. 7:12.
[8] 1 Cor. 3:21–23.
[9] Mt. 10:8.
[10] 2 Tim. 2:10.
[11] Lk. 17:10.
[12] *Way of Perfection*, IV, 4.

Notes for Chapter Fifteen

[1] Jn. 8:44.
[2] *Ascent of Mt. Carmel*, VI:7.
[3] *Summa Theol.*, I, q. 109, a. 2.
[4] 1 Pet. 5:8.
[5] Ps. 112:4–6.
[6] Cf. Isa. 57:15.
[7] Isa. 66:1, 2.
[8] Num. 12:8.
[9] Num. 12:3.
[10] Ecclus. 3:20, 21.
[11] Mt. 18:4.
[12] Mt. 23:12.
[13] Mt. 11:29.
[14] Mt. 10:24; Jn. 13:13.
[15] Jn. 13:15, 17.
[16] Cf. Jer. 49, 16 ff.
[17] Prov. 11:2.
[18] Ps. 36:35, 36.
[19] Gen. 1:28.
[20] Cf. 2 Cor. 5:8.
[21] Jn. 17:24.

22 *Summa Theol.*, I, q. LXIII, a. 2.
23 1 Cor. 1:31.
24 Mt. 19:17; 18:3.
25 *Avisos:* aviso 326.
26 1 Cor. 4:7.
27 *Avisos:* aviso 327.
28 Prov. 14:30.
29 *Avisos:* aviso 327.

NOTES FOR CHAPTER SIXTEEN

1 Hab. 2:5.
2 Ecclus. 31:35, 36.
3 Ps. 81:6.
4 Mt. 4:9.
5 Mt. 23:26.
6 Cf. Ps. 73:23.
7 Hab. 2:5.
8 Prov. 20:9.
9 Ecclus. 31:31.
10 *Ascent of Mt. Carmel*, III, VIII:2.
11 *Avisos:* aviso 329.
12 Rom. 7:1.
13 Cf. Jn. 4:24.
14 *Way of Perfection*, XII, 6.
15 *Avisos:* aviso 231.

NOTES FOR CHAPTER SEVENTEEN

1 *La Santidad*, XVII:334.
2 1 Cor. 13:5.
3 *Ibid.*, 4, 5, 7.
4 *Avisos:* aviso 178.
5 *Ibid.*, 334.
6 Mt. 10:30, 31.
7 Cf. Rom. 8:28.
8 1 Thess. 4:3.
9 2 Kings 16:10, 12.
10 Letter XVI, to M. Maria of the Incarnation.
11 *Interior Castle*, III:5.
12 *La Santidad*, XVII, 360.
13 *Avisos:* aviso 179.
14 *La Santidad*, XVII: 361.

NOTES FOR CHAPTER EIGHTEEN

1 *La Santidad*, XVIII, 364.
2 Cf. Ecclus. 2:10.
3 Cf. 3 Kings 11:7.
4 Cf. Ps. 80:13.
5 Ps. 80:12, 13.

[6] 1 Cor. 2:14.
[7] *Ascent of Mt. Carmel*, I, IV, 2.
[8] *Ibid.*, 6:3.
[9] Isa. 57:20, 21.
[10] *Ascent of Mt. Carmel*, I, IV, 8.
[11] Isa. 29:8.
[12] Job 20:22, 27.
[13] Jer. 2:24.
[14] *Ascent of Mt. Carmel*, XIX, 5.
[15] *Ibid.*, 8:2.
[16] *Avisos:* aviso 34.
[17] *Ibid.*, aviso 17.
[18] *Ascent of Mt. Carmel*, XIX, 5.
[19] *Ibid.*, 27:5.
[20] Lk. 10:3.
[21] Lk. 10:17, 19, 20.
[22] *Avisos:* aviso 38.
[23] *Ascent of Mt. Carmel*, III, XXV, 2.
[24] Mt. 19:29.
[25] *Ascent of Mt. Carmel*, III, XXVI, 289.
[26] Gal. 2:19.
[27] Phil. 1:21.

NOTES FOR CHAPTER NINETEEN

[1] *La Santidad*, XIX, 388.
[2] *Ascent of Mt. Carmel*, I, XIII, 3.
[3] *Ibid.*, 56.
[4] *Summa Theol.*, I, II, q. XXXIX, a. 1.
[5] Apoc. 18:7.
[6] Mt. 12:36, 37.
[7] Ps. 39:13.
[8] Rom. 14:12.
[9] 1 Cor. 3:13.
[10] Ecclus. 2:22.
[11] Lk. 12:58, 59.
[12] Col. 1:24.
[13] *Dark Night of the Soul*, X, 5.
[14] *Ibid.*, XII:1.
[15] 2 Par. 34:27.
[16] Wisd. 3:4.
[17] Cf. 2 Tim. 1:12.
[18] Ecclus. 4:9, 11.
[19] Isa. 54:10, 11.
[20] Rom. 8:29, 30.
[21] Mk. 8:34.
[22] Mt. 10:38.
[23] Phil. 1:29.
[24] *Avisos:* aviso 85, 87.
[25] Gal. 6:14.
[26] Letter VII to Sr. Juana de Pedraza.
[27] *Interior Life*, II, Relation 34.

28 Isa. 53:3.
29 Lk. 9:62.
30 Mt. 11:12.
31 Gal. 3:3.
32 *La Santidad*, XIX, 415.
33 *Spiritual Canticle*, XXXVI, 11.
34 Mk. 8:4, 5.
35 *Ascent of Mt. Carmel*, VI:4.

NOTES FOR CHAPTER TWENTY

1 *Ascent of Mt. Carmel*, Prologue, 15.
2 *La Santidad*, XX, 421.
3 *Avisos: aviso* 152.
4 3 Kings 18:3.
5 *Way of Perfection*, XL:4.
6 *Dark Night of the Soul*, VI, 365.
7 *Ibid.*, II:6.
8 2 Cor. 5:14.
9 *Foundations*, I:6, 7.
10 *Ibid.*, I, 10, 11.
11 *La Santidad*, XX, 439.
12 *Avisos:* prologue.
13 *Ibid.*
14 1 Cor. 13:2.
15 *Avisos: aviso* 21.
16 *Avisos: aviso* 33, 38.
17 *History of a Soul*, VII.

NOTES FOR CHAPTER TWENTY-ONE

1 *Avisos:* prologue.
2 *Ibid.*, 27, 28.
3 *Ibid.*, 127.
4 Cf. Mt. 10:38.
5 Mt. 5:48.
6 1 Tim. 2:5; Hebr. 13:8.
7 Cf. Jn. 14:6.
8 *Avisos: aviso* 77.
9 Cf. Lk. 12:28.
10 Cf. Mt. 10:30.
11 Lk. 6:37.
12 Lk. 6:31.

NOTES FOR CHAPTER TWENTY-TWO

1 Ecclus. 24:14, 16.
2 Cf. Rom. 12:2.
3 Cf. Rom. 8:3.
4 Rom. 8:38, 39.
5 *Ascent of Mt. Carmel*, I.

6 Dark Night of the Soul, VI:365.
7 La Santidad, XII, 244.
8 Avisos: aviso 237.
9 Ascent of Mt. Carmel, II, VII, 3.
10 Ibid.
11 Lk. 14:26.